Dying To Be Immortal

Man's Journey Back to Eden

The Eden Chronicles, LLC
P.O. Box 697
Concord, NH 03302
www.edenchronicles.org

Editing, layout and production by Julie K. Andrés
Blue Moon Publishing / www.bluemoonpublishing.ca

Cover design and interior illustrations: Jeannette E. Waugh

Printed in Canada

ISBN: 978-0-9881789-0-8

Brown, Daniel J.

    Dying to be immortal: man's journey back to Eden / Daniel J. Brown

Dying To Be Immortal

MAN'S JOURNEY BACK TO EDEN

Daniel J. Brown

The Eden Chronicles
Concord, NH

To all who have the courage to embark on the
challenging yet exciting journey
back to Eden.

CONTENTS

Part V
Adam and Eve's Addiction to the Forbidden Fruit

Part VI
The Journey Home

Introduction

Why I Wrote This Book

I have written this book for every immortal soul. I wish to awaken in every soul a remembrance of the intimate bonds of love that unite us and of the timeless life we once enjoyed in the eternal Paradise called Eden. I hope to awaken the memory of the journey we were supposed to take and contrast it with the detour that has cost us all so dearly. However, awakening that memory will first require a reexamination of certain long and deeply held beliefs. The foundation of those beliefs is the supposition that throughout all of creation man stands uniquely alone as the culminating event in God's wondrous creation. It is a conviction of faith that declares that it is only man who was created in the image and after the likeness of God. Throughout this book, I will identify that image and likeness of God as the Atom of God Consciousness.

Genesis in a Nutshell

In the creation story of Genesis we learn that man became a living soul clothed with a physical body. The soul has always been an enigma to man. In this book, I will propose that the soul is the energy and substance of light that clothes everything that emanates out of the Consciousness of God. In Genesis we discover that man was created as a threefold being, first emanating out of the Consciousness of God as spirit, as an Atom of God Consciousness. Man as spirit was then clothed with a garment woven with the energy substance of light. This garment of light is the soul. Man, as spirit and soul, was then further clothed with a garment fashioned from physical matter, from the dust of the ground. This physical garment is the body.

The Enigma of the Soul

Everything within creation is composed of body, soul, and spirit. However, throughout the infinite expanse that we call creation, it is only the soul covering worn by man that was uniquely formed.

The soul covering worn by man was uniquely fashioned when God placed his breath into the nostrils of the physical body of the man, Adam. When the soul breath of God was poured into the physical body of Adam, man became an individualized soul, a living soul, an immortal soul. Within the Paradise called Eden, it is only man who is clothed with an immortal soul body. The physical body of man, his body of dust, now magnetized around an immortal soul body, becomes imperishable and will never be subject to death or decay. This inexhaustible breath of God, given only to man, creates a unique relationship between man and his Creator, a relationship enjoyed by no other living being.

Man's Relationship with God Need Not Be Elusive

There is nothing else within all of creation equal to man. Yet, and notwithstanding the numerous religious doctrines that have existed throughout the long history of man's existence, the reality of man as an immortal child of God continues to remain elusive and ill-defined. Unfortunately, the various religious sects have almost always spoken more to the rules of membership and to an inflexible dogma than to that much greater reality of man as a true Child of God. Equally as significant has been the lack of a meaningful and embraceable discussion on the imperishable garment of light called the immortal soul, man's corruption of that garment, and his exile from Eden.

It was as a result of the inability of religion to speak more directly regarding such profound matters that, as a young man, I was led to seriously question the capacity of any religious doctrine to provide man with a genuine path of redemption—a path that could clearly lead man back home to the timeless Paradise of Eden. Searching for such a path has taken me on a fascinating metaphysical journey. It has been a journey leading out of the confines of nature and into an intangible expanse where I have experienced what I will refer to as the light substance of consciousness. While in this field of light, my conscious awareness was not contained as if within a body or brain, but was wholly unbounded—so much so that I felt my presence to be as large as the expanse that I occupied. My experiences within this realm of light have brought me closer to an understanding of the presence and power we call God, of man's divine and immortal nature, and of the true cause of man's fall and exile from the Paradise of Eden.

The Foundation of All Reality Is Consciousness

Man presently lacks an understanding of the full power of what we call consciousness. We do not appreciate that what we call the experience of life is nothing other than an experience within and of the energy of consciousness. The energy of consciousness is the foundation of the reality we identify as nature. Moreover, it is also the foundation of infinite realities that lie beyond our present level of conscious perception and awareness. One's experience within this infinite energy field of consciousness is determined by the level or degree to which one is consciously self-aware. The degree or level of self-awareness also determines whether our so-called experience of life is actually real or just an illusionary dream. For most of humanity, the experience is but a dream.

As I have journeyed through life, I have found that my experience of living within nature is akin to living within the reflection of a mirror. To my physical senses, what I observe while moving through nature appears like one large and neatly assorted arrangement of silk flowers, representative of something real, but itself not real. And although my physical senses tell me that the assorted arrangement of silk flowers are indeed real, there nevertheless remains a deep sense that something about my relationship with nature is not quite right, or natural. It is a relational experience more like that of a visitor to a foreign country who, unfamiliar with the local customs or language, feels uncomfortable and out of place. It is a relationship that is both benignly indifferent, yet inescapably necessary. Notwithstanding the quality of our relationship, there remains the sense that we are each but a reflection wholly contained within the projected image of the mirror, and that our reflections are hiding a much greater truth.

As eloquent as our language can be, words are nevertheless inadequate to describe what we can experience when stepping through the reflective veil of nature and into the infinite expanse of consciousness. The best way I can describe the experience is to liken it to waking up while in a state of sleep. You know your body remains comfortably asleep, yet you are fully awake, free and detached from your sleeping body. Furthermore, you discover that while in that free and detached state you are able to think in a creative and systematic manner not typically experienced in the so-called waking state. In that state, the activity of thinking is like the pleasant and gentle movement of a summer breeze. By comparison, the manner of thinking experienced while moving within the mirror image of nature is passive, sensory-induced, and dreamlike. Furthermore, within the reflection of nature there appears the endless cycle of days and nights, of beginnings and endings, brought about as our state of conscious awareness waxes and wanes. Yet, when stepping out of the reflective image of nature and into the expanse of Consciousness you feel your presence no longer bound by the contours of a physical body. You become aware that while in this expanse you experience time differently. You no longer feel like you are being carried along, as if on a rising wave you cannot stop or control. You feel as though you are the wave with the power to alter and change course at will. There is only the experience of the bonded unity between the thinker, the thoughts created, and the light substance of consciousness in which both are contained. The overall experience is like that of a timeless day being enjoyed by a timeless and immortal consciousness. It is like knowing with an unquestionable certainty that the best day you have ever had will never end. You feel as though you have returned to a warm, comforting place that you have been to many times before, a place forgotten while asleep in the dream of life. Anyone who chooses to turn off his physical senses and to step through the mirror will also experience what I have described above.

Sensually Versus Consciously Created Thoughts

However, so long as we remain asleep in the dream of life, we will also remain ignorant of the foundational knowledge that when we think we are using the energy of consciousness to create our reality. We do not currently appreciate that when we think we are using the energy of consciousness, like a potter's clay, to fashion our thoughts. Nor do we understand that, once created our thoughts will exist forever as they have been formed with the indestructible energy of consciousness. Once created, our many thoughts not only have an independent existence bonding together to form our personally unique and individual reality, they also form part of and help shape the greater world reality we collectively share. Yet, for most of us, our thoughts are not self-consciously created as much as they are formed through the interplay of our physical senses when activated through our intercourse with nature. The result is our thinking and the thoughts we create are most often simply the product of a passive response to external stimuli. Over the course of my journey it has become clear to me that the experience we call life, like a coin, has two sides. On one side we find the energy of consciousness being fashioned into infinite and varied forms of thought as spirit. On the other we find these varied forms of thought, of spirit, evolving and taking on the denser energetic clothing of physical matter. Each, are nevertheless, inseparably bonded, one to the other.

It is this concept of the bonded union between spirit and matter forming the foundational underpinnings for all reality that I invite every reader to explore. However, such an undertaking will require looking at our temporal life experience from a perspective that will unquestionably be at odds with current orthodox social, scientific, and religious belief systems. The existing paradigm, forged in great part by an incomplete scientific and religious construct, has become strained against the ever-expanding conscious and psychic development of mankind. It is a paradigm of thought that for centuries has had as its foundation the twin pillars of fear and repression. It is a paradigm that has proven to be inadequate in advancing man's comprehension of his divine immortal soul and how it has become inextricably interwoven with his temporal physical nature.

The Failure of the Marriage Between Science and Religion

Throughout the long millennia of man's existence, both science and religion have been unable to provide definitive answers to questions pertaining to the origin of man and of the universe he occupies. Nor has either comprehensively addressed the question of whether man and his universe have not only a material origin, but a spiritual one as well. Science disavows the relevance of a God in its search for answers to such profound questions. Instead it relies on a methodology that employs gathering and assessing empirical, measurable data, contending that to be the only rational method for understanding man and the universe he occupies. However, despite the efforts of the greatest minds of science, they have been unable to close the circle of understanding on what we call our physical material reality.

Likewise, religion disavows the relevance of science in what it perceives as spiritual, non-temporal matters, contending that questions pertaining to man's origin, and that of the universe, involve matters of faith. The world's principal religions proclaim a belief in one Supreme Being, one God, responsible for all creation. However, despite the belief in a universal creator, there has been throughout history a competition among the religious sects of the world as to which among their numbers truly speaks for the one and only God.

The unfortunate consequence of such competition has been to make God into the "image and likeness" of man, fostering throughout man's long history unnecessary, and oftentimes violent, conflicts with unholy results. The religions of the world have proven inadequate in providing man with an embraceable understanding of that profound reality we call God, of man's origin and evolution, and of man's relationship to God. What the religions of the world fail to understand is that as an all-encompassing universal reality, God cannot be coopted by any one religious denomination.

It is Time for All Souls to Awaken

Dying to be Immortal is about a soul's awakening to the unity of life as an experience of consciousness as it expands and unfolds within the material realm of nature. It speaks to a soul's awakening to the realization of why we find ourselves living as if within the reflection of a mirror—more akin to a virtual reality—and how we may be able to exit this virtual reality and return home to the Paradise of Eden. It is not my intention to offer definitive statements on modern day science, comparative religions, or studies in consciousness. I will not engage the reader in existential mind stretching or the minutiae of scientific investigation. For those who may be interested in such endeavors, there are other numerous and excellent sources available, some of which I have recommended at the end of this book.

This book simply offers a discussion of whether the scientific and religious paradigm of life by which we have been guided for so long has been successful in truly advancing man's understanding of his divine immortal nature and how it relates to his temporal life experience. I believe we desperately need to create a new paradigm, a different way of viewing the relationship between spirit and matter—the divine and the temporal—more befitting our modern, expanding level of conscious and psychic awareness.

Hopefully, this book will spur a concerted effort in each of us to explore a new model, a new paradigm, of consciousness to aid man in his journey back to the world to which he truly belongs, and which, in reality, he has never left. For without a new direction, man will continue to cycle through lives of violence and war as if in an endless time loop, never returning to the paradise for which he so desperately yearns. With but a little effort, we all can awaken a remembrance of the timeless, immortal life we once enjoyed and the reason why we faltered so badly. With an awakened consciousness we will then be able to better fashion a model by which we can successfully complete our return home to the timeless Paradise of Eden.

PART I

The Failure of a Paradigm

Is There No One to Point the Way?

~

Science Fails to See Matter as the Clothing Worn by Spirit

Scientists theorize that our universe began in one infinitesimal nano-second of time with an incomprehensible explosion. This singular event, which gave rise to the creation of the universe, has been characterized as the Big Bang theory of creation. The origination for this theory is based on certain assumptions arrived at by an examination of the perceived size of the universe and how its size correlates with the speed at which light travels. An analysis of the mass of the universe and the speed of light led scientists to conclude that our universe was initially an infinitely compressed body of matter. And that within that tightly compacted body of matter temperature rose to such a degree that its energy ignited a violent expansion. The expansion of this primordial matter has, over the course of an estimated 13 billion years, resulted in the formation of an incalculable number of planets, stars, and galaxies, all contained within an envelope of space and time called the universe.

However, this Big Bang theory fails to answer the question as to the origin or composition of that initial body of primordial matter or the source of the underlying energy that it came to interact with to create a universe reality that, after 13 billion years, continues to expand. Science has confirmed that the universe had a pronounced beginning. However, it cannot say whether the universe arose out of a primordial super atom, making the universe one of a kind—an only child—or whether our universe was born out of a larger meta-universe making our universe perhaps but one sibling among many. To date, science has simply been unable to solve the mystery surrounding the genesis of the Big Bang.

There have been some highly intelligent minds that, contemplating the phenomenal creation of the universe, have been led to theorize that there was an apparent intelligent design at work—a creative hand, so to speak. One to whom such an intelligent design theory was apparent was Sir Isaac Newton (1642-1727). Newton was a highly respected physicist, mathematician, and natural philosopher; he is considered to be one of the most important scientists of all time. He laid the groundwork for classical mechanics, or the view that the universe is a finely created and tuned machine. Newton further believed that not only was there a maker of this machine, but, of necessity, someone who kept the machine tuned and smoothly operating. His views in that regard were not then, and are not now, embraced by the broader scientific community.

Intelligent design is the general notion that all substance, objects, and events playing out in the universe are all formed and acted upon by that very same energy that brought them into existence. Science tells us that the total amount of energy within the envelope of our universe remains constant and that; although it can be changed from one form to another, this energy can neither be increased nor destroyed. Therefore, we can reasonably anticipate that the energy comprising our universe will continue to exist forever, nevertheless expressing itself in diversified ways. We can likewise reasonably assume that man, also being made up of energy, an energy that also embodies a constituent characteristic of self-conscious awareness, will exist forever, in one form or another, as self-conscious energy.

The relevant question therefore becomes: what are the inherent qualities or characteristics of the energy that brought the phenomenal universe into existence? Does such energy contain within its matrix a grand unifying element common to all matter within the universe? The reluctance of science to embrace any concept suggestive of a conscious design as a characteristic inherent within the energy matrix of all matter has brought its efforts of reducing the properties of matter to a point beyond which it can go no further. Enter the quantum physicists, with mathematical theories as to the hidden nature of matter that our senses cannot detect, but that they intuitively believe exists. Despite their best efforts, the quantum physicists have been unable to unlock the mystery hidden in the bonded union between energy and matter. We continue to be left with the prevailing view that the diversity and complexity of physical matter found within our universe evolved out of a series of random and chaotic acts. However, such a view strains our comprehension.

Everything contained within the envelope of our universe arose out of the coalescence of matter around an energetic 'blueprint'." All matter exists and is made perceptible by its coalescence around a diverse and limitless variety of archetypal forms composed of energy. This coalescence of matter and archetypal forms is so unique that not even the pattern of two snowflakes are exactly alike. This bonding of matter and energy makes the universe perceptible to us. However, should we assume that energy and matter exist only within our envelope of space and time? We believe that both matter and energy existed prior to the Big Bang and that it was the result of an interactive union between the two that has given us our universe. However, we find ourselves limited in an understanding of the pre-Big Bang reality simply because we cannot yet clearly see within the envelope that is our universe.

For some time physicists have been engaged in a study of the quantum field, that energetic canvas upon which the material universe is impressed. In Genesis, the first book of the Bible, this field is called the firmament (Genesis 1:6, Douay-Rheims Version). Collectively, this quantum field is formed of the underlying energy, the glue that holds together our physical material universe. However, physicists have yet to discover the unifying character of that energetic glue, or whether that glue might also exist outside of our envelope of time, space, and matter.

Any discussion as to the existence and quality of a quantum field brings us once again to questions of origin--intelligent or otherwise. Who or what is responsible for the incomprehensible scale, diversity, and complexity of both man and the universe? Who or what continues to maintain what we believe to be the mathematical precision of the universe? Perhaps such questions will always remain beyond man's capacity to satisfactorily answer. We can certainly theorize, and within the exercise of theorizing we may find the answer or at least be pointed in the right direction.

For example, we can all agree that man, composed of both energy and matter, is also a self-conscious being. Is man's consciousness a physical function possible only when aided by the operation of his physical brain and occurring only when he is encapsulated within the envelope of time and space? Or does consciousness transcend the human physical condition as well as time and space? I will not only argue that it does, but that the energy of consciousness is itself the unifying element common to all matter, whether within or outside of our perceptible universe. Without the energy of consciousness, man would not only be unaware of his existence. He and the universe would not exist.

The 'who' or 'what' responsible for the incomprehensible scale, complexity, and diversity of both man and the universe is the energy of consciousness. Consciousness is that inexhaustible and unbounded energy within which we find the matrix of everything that has or could ever possibly come into material existence. Consciousness is the primordial energy connecting all possible realities whether, presently perceptible to us or not. There is no reality greater than that of consciousness. It has no origin, no creator. It simply has always existed as energy. You can call this foundational energy the Quantum Field, the First Cause, the Supreme Being, or God. Throughout this book, I call this underlying energy, the infinite pure Consciousness of God. We have to understand that the consciousness experienced by man, although originating out of the energy that is the infinite pure Consciousness of God, is not itself pure consciousness. As a drop of water is to an ocean, so is man's conscious awareness when compared to the infinite sea of consciousness from which he has emerged. Moreover, man's use of the inexhaustible energy of consciousness is hampered by his over-reliance on the physical bodily sensors as a means of discerning reality. As a result, man is more asleep than conscious, even when he believes himself to be awake. Living as if in a never-ending dream has hindered man's ability to fully understand his own unique reality, let alone the greater reality of which he is a part.

In their search for an all-unifying principle connecting all physical matter within the universe, physicists have been successful in reducing the constituent particles of physical matter—the atoms and molecules that make up matter—to the point where they observe space between particles. This raises the obvious question: What is holding physical matter together? Matter is defined in physics as that which occupies space and possesses mass. Might not the space between these particles of physical matter itself be made up of a form and density of matter different perhaps only in degree and character than we are presently acquainted with? The answer is yes. The space existing between the constituent particles of physical matter is, like the particles themselves, made up of the energy and substance of consciousness. Consciousness is that energetic glue that not only holds our universe together, but is also the substance out of which all form and manner of creation flows. The space between the particles of physical matter is composed of threads of consciousness that, when woven together, form the clothing ensemble worn by all material objects.

Simply stated, everything emerges out of an infinite sea of energy, the waters of which are pure consciousness. It is an unalterable sea of energy unaffected by all the many and varied manifestations of consciousness that emerge out of it. Until science recognizes that the energy of consciousness is the foundational component out of which our material universe not only has come into being, but by which it will, in one form or another, remain, it will continue to seek answers to the profound mysteries of life with one hand tied behind its back.

The science of Newton and Einstein has reached its limits in its attempts to determine the look of the reality from which our material universe emerged. Science fails to recognize that there is an inherent design principle within the energy of consciousness, operating as a universal law that is responsible for the diversity found within creation. I will refer to that inherent design principle, that animating and vital principle, as the spirit of consciousness. More importantly, this animating spirit principle of the energy of Consciousness is foundational for the continued existence of all matter, no matter what form it may take. Yet, science has so elevated the importance of matter in the search for that one unifying principle holding the universe together that it has blinded itself to any vision of the role of spirit in that union. As a result, the greatest minds of science taking on such inquiry will remain unable to discover the underlying principle that unites all material things within our universe and our universe within the greater reality of its origin.

The fact of the matter is the Big Bang theory falls short of closing the circle on our understanding of creation and man's place or purpose within it. Although this theory allows for the backward extrapolation of observable data, it does so only up to that theoretical infinitesimal nanosecond of time when the Big Bang occurred. Prior to that point, no further data can be obtained because our instruments of discovery are not yet advanced enough, or, if they are, because what they disclose to us is yet beyond the grasp of our comprehension. What we see we cannot yet recognize.

Quantum physics, as it moves closer to metaphysics, will eventually cross the threshold of man's present understanding and discover that our physical world is the offspring of a transcendent, non-material, and yes, incomprehensible reality. I say it is an incomprehensible reality, as man can never fully know or comprehend that which is greater than himself, at least not solely with the temporal mind guided only by the physical senses. In crossing the threshold, science will peer into a world that, like ours, is composed of both matter and spirit. It will discover that the underlying and unifying principle between the seen world of matter, and unseen world of spirit, is in fact a union or marriage of the two.

Religion Fails to See the Evolution of Spirit within Matter

Genesis, the Bible story of creation, is an allegorical presentation of cosmic and transcendent events. An allegory is defined as a story that can be interpreted to reveal a hidden meaning. Yet man, having consistently placed too literal an interpretation on the story of creation, has sacrificed the hidden meaning contained therein. As a consequence, man has avoided the exciting inquiry as to whether his origin was first in a world of spirit as the Atom of God Consciousness or in a world of matter as the physical Adam. Or, whether one might simply be an evolution of the other.

Genesis tells us that all of creation occurred through the Spoken Word of God. God said, "let there be..." and so it was. Creationists take that statement at face value believing, as is reported in Genesis, in the instantaneous manifestation of the heaven and the earth populated with a diverse variety of life, including man—all in a matter of six days. Unfortunately, neither Genesis nor the creationists provide any meaningful insight into that reality out of which our physical world emerged. Nor does either provide any particular insight into our understanding of whom or what God is, or why God was moved to create.

Believing Genesis to be an allegorical presentation of creation, what meaning are we to attribute to the Spoken Word of God? God, being a reality greater than the collective sum of all his creations, would not, like man, be contained within any form, and least of all within a physical material body. God would not require a mouth or vocal cords in order to communicate. So how would God speak? The sound that is the Spoken Word of God arises out of an energetic and dynamic movement occurring within the infinite sea of pure consciousness. We can view this dynamic movement as being similar to the movement occurring within man's field of consciousness when triggered by the activity of thinking. However, the activity of thinking engaged in by man does not adequately capture the dynamic movement that we refer to as the Spoken Word of God. There just are no adequate words to describe such activity occurring within the infinite Consciousness of God. Such activity is neither conceived, formulated, nor contemplated. Nor is it labored or prone to error, but is always perfect when issued. The energetic and dynamic movement that is the Spoken Word of God leads to the evolution of the energy of consciousness as it takes on the garments, the layers and substance of matter. Because man limits the depth of his vision to what he can observe through his five physical senses, he excludes the possible existence of other realities that, by comparison to our temporal world, would appear non-material in composition. Man's conscious awareness being so restrained has prevented him from discovering that he has additional and more sensitive senses that, if accessed, would readily allow him to perceive such other finer material realities. An embrace of the possible existence of such higher senses of consciousness would certainly make the reality of Eden, as well as of God, more embraceable by the mind of man.

However, contemplating such theories requires the acceptance of a methodology that looks more deeply into the allegorical presentation of cosmic and transcendent events. Creationists do not recognize as an integral process of creation the gradual systematic and evolutionary advancement of spirit as it takes on the clothing of matter. By elevating creationism over a more gradual methodical evolution of spirit within matter, religion has excluded any potential for seeing the full breadth or Consciousness of God at work, and therefore stops at the threshold of the bridge that connects spirit with matter.

Let us for a moment contemplate the purpose and relevancy of our infinite universe within God's overall plan of creation. If man is the one and only personal representative of God, and exists only on the planet Earth, then the obvious question is why would God create such a fantastic universe whose reality is beyond man's capacity to fully comprehend, let alone to fully experience? It is highly questionable whether man will ever develop the means to leave his own solar system, let alone traverse his own galaxy. Man cannot anticipate ever exploring the billions of other galaxies that we know exist in the universe. Despite man's incredible intellectual and technological advancements, we lack the ability to determine the actual size or scale of the universe, whether there is only one universe, or whether our universe may be but a meta-galaxy within an even larger incomprehensible meta-universe.

Scientists tell us that light from the most distant stars in the universe, traveling at the speed of light, has taken billions of years to reach a point in the vastness of space to be seen by our most advanced telescopes. Yet we cannot with an absolute certainty say whether the stars that cast the light that we can now observe still exist, since the distance is so incomprehensibly great that we cannot see the actual stars. Although man has improved his telescopes and thereby expanded the universe, he still is unaware of its actual size or attributes. Even with the Hubble Telescope, one of the most advanced and versatile telescopes ever created, man is still limited as to what he can see through its lenses. For all we know, beyond the vision of Hubble lay billions of other universes. Even creationists must wonder at the scale and purpose of what we perceive as our physical universe. Our universe is nothing short of an extension of the transcendent and eternal, materialized into physical form. As the skeleton, muscles, and flesh of the human body clothe the spirit of man, so too are the transcendent and eternal realities clothed by the body of the manifest infinite universe.

However, instead of exploring such cosmic and transcendent concepts, man, with his limited capacity for comprehension of all things greater than himself, has found it easier to personalize his conception of God. Man was created "in the image and after the likeness" of God, so obviously God is like us. In personalizing God, we effectively limit the wonder of the infinite as it unfolds in its movement through that greater reality that is the Consciousness of God. Religion must move beyond this childlike personalization of God, much as science must move beyond the belief that a world that cannot be seen, measured, or tested does not exist.

One hundred years after the Theory of Relativity and two thousand years after the message of Christ, man still clings to outdated traditions and flawed thinking. Science has given us tremendous technological achievements but has yet to discover the essence of our humanity. Religion, despite the beacon light of the Christ, has slipped further into over-reliance on man-made rules and dogma such that we no longer are able to hear the soft voice of God that resides within each of us.

Genesis has been for religion what the Big Bang has been for science; a theoretical starting point from which man has been able to move forward but not backward in his search for the ultimate truth. Science, in its failure to embrace the transcendent as real, has hindered the ability of man to discover the connective link unifying everything within and without our universe. Religion, in its failure to accept this temporal physical experience as an unbroken extension of the greater transcendent spiritual reality, has hindered the ability of man to experience his own divinity. The continued embrace by science and religion of their respective worldviews and of man's place within them will continue to stifle man's redemption and his return home to the Paradise of Eden.

Both science and religion need to understand that matter and spirit form a unified reality. We are not there yet, so let us enjoy this conversation in which we contemplate the possibilities of our origin, both divine and temporal. The time has come to try something different, to step out of the restrictions and limitations imposed by science and religion, and to fashion a new paradigm of thought that will catapult humanity on its journey back to Eden.

The Elusive Redemption of Man

Man clearly sees himself as standing at the pinnacle of all creation. Nothing else within nature, or elsewhere in the universe, has ever challenged man's apparent supremacy. Yet despite man's elevated station, he has yet to demonstrate that he truly understands the profound mysteries of his own creation, his relationship with God, or his placement within a universe so vast as to be beyond his comprehension. It is indisputable that over time, man's self-conscious and psychic awareness has gone through a phenomenal evolution. However, man's consideration of the profound mysteries surrounding his origin—and of his experience within the reality called life—continues to remain childlike.

This is due, in part, to the fact that for millennia man has been trapped in a childlike paradigm of fear fostered by the belief that his Creator is an angry and violent God. We first witness the anger of God in the story of man's creation as told in Genesis. After God learns that his children, Adam and Eve, had eaten the fruit of the Tree of Knowledge, the fruit that he commanded that they not eat, he not only strips them of their physical immortality, but he expels them from the Paradise of Eden (Genesis 3:23). This act of disobedience by Adam and Eve has become universally known as the "Original Sin." Here "original" is understood to mean "first," while "sin" can be understood as an action or transgression that is highly reprehensible.

Once exiled from Eden, the transgressions or sins of man increased so dramatically that an angry God declared, "... [he] was sorry that he had made man on the earth... I will blot out man whom I have created from the face of the land, man and animals and creeping things and birds of the heavens, for I am sorry that I have made them" (Genesis 6:6-7). God caused a great flood to roll across the face of the Earth, destroying all life except for the "...generations of Noah who was a righteous man..." (Genesis 6-8). The great flood was later followed by the total destruction of the cities of Sodom and Gomorrah. These cities, along with everyone in them, were consumed by fire and brimstone because the Angels of God could not find at least ten righteous men living within them (Genesis 18:22-33; 19:1-29).

It is not just rage and anger, but, according to the writings of the Old Testament, God is also prone to jealousy—"there shall be no other Gods but me (Exodus 20:3) and demands adulation—"you must make offerings to me of the crops of your fields, and animals of your herds: (Exodus 22:29-30). Man, being incapable of comprehending the reality of God, has made God into the image and likeness of man—a jealous, angry, and violent overseer. As a result, such men, ignorant of their own divine nature, are not only warring against each other, but against God as well. The creation of this paradigm of fear has hampered man's search not only for the divine within himself, but within the greater creation of which he is but a part.

To our collective consciousness God has been portrayed in such a way as to cause man to live not in the certainty that upon death a warm homecoming awaits him, but in fear of a frightful and inescapable judgment. This fear of God has been astutely advanced and managed by those social, political, and religious forces that, through the millennia, have sought to control the thoughts and actions of humanity. Even as I write these words, there are many prominent public figures in America asserting that the violent and devastating floods, tornados, hurricanes, droughts, and earthquakes that are occurring all over our planet are punishments from God. These public figures contend that the seemingly unending global and catastrophic punishments are a direct result of man's deviation from the rules and commandments handed down by God. And, not surprisingly, these same public figures claim that by adopting their favored social policies we can placate God and end the plague of punishments.

Such a paradigm of fear fosters within the minds of man a dreadful apprehension of a God whom we have been led to believe must always be placated. It is a paradigm that puts forth the notion that, as the descendants of Adam and Eve, we are all tainted by their original sin. It is a confusing paradigm of thought that holds that only through the redemption of our immortal soul, created by God yet born in sin, can we hope to ever again enjoy the loving embrace of God. The path to redemption remains not only ill defined and therefore elusive, but has become so great a burden as to seem impossible to achieve. As a consequence, we continue to fear death and the inevitable punishment from God that we believe will surely follow.

Unfortunately, Genesis leaves us with far more questions than answers. We are not told anything about this God of Genesis or of the nature of his relationship with Adam and Eve. There is no commentary as to why God endows Adam and Eve with the freedom of choice, yet imposes a limitation on their exercise of that freedom. Although Adam and Eve are told of the consequences of eating the fruit of the Tree of Knowledge—"thou shalt surely die"—there is no explanation as to why this particular tree was placed in Eden. And, more astonishingly, what are we to make of the tempter within Eden? A serpent among the "beasts of the field" that could walk, talk and apparently overcome the higher consciousness of the children of God?

Genesis leaves us pondering why God would impose such a harsh and unremitting punishment not only upon Adam and Eve, but more importantly, upon all of their descendants, generation after generation. Does the punishment of expelling Adam and Eve from the light of Paradise into a world of darkness, while also dimming awareness of their divine origin, really fit the crime? Is the God of Genesis truly so unforgiving? If Genesis gives us an accurate picture of God as prone to anger and quick to punish, then man has good reason to fear his Creator. The story of Genesis should, but unfortunately does not, nourish the soul of man.

Perhaps it is because Genesis does not offer man the soothing elixir of God's love that man, through the long and dusty march of civilization, has continued to live a life of astonishing imperfection. We have been told that the path of our redemption for that "original sin" committed by Adam and Eve, and which, as their descendants, we cannot escape, is quite simple: Live a good and moral life and you will be rewarded with eternal life in Paradise. There is even a 'golden rule' to guide us that states, "As you wish that men would do to you, do so to them" (Luke 6:13). Yet despite the simplicity of this golden rule, man has, throughout the centuries, and in the most inconceivable of ways, continued to brutalize one another, often doing so in the name of God.

How can it be that, despite a universal belief in God and in a paradise called Heaven, man has so miserably failed to secure for himself a clearly defined path of redemption? Maybe we have it all wrong. Maybe it is not a matter of making it all right with the God of Genesis. Although we acknowledge the reality of a Supreme Being responsible for our creation, our understanding of our relationship to that Supreme Being is, at best, clouded. Perhaps our clouded understanding is simply the result of our fall and exile from Eden, and the resulting consequences of that fall and exile have nothing to do with concepts of punishment or retribution. Perhaps it is simply a case that, by his actions in Eden, man alone has created his own world of pain and suffering.

The fall of Adam and Eve has had inescapable consequences that each of us must personally confront if we are ever to restore ourselves to that previous state of imperishable perfection that we enjoyed in the Paradise of Eden. We can call that effort redemption. However, man's redemption is a journey that has nothing to do with punishment, at least not a punishment imposed by God. Redemption is simply the process by which each of us travels through this world of time, space, and matter, striving to reclaim our full potential as the immortal children of God we were created to be.

Man lives in ignorance of the reality that is God. We sorely need a better model to define our understanding of and relationship with God, our fall from grace, and the reason why our redemption has been so elusive. We need to be done with a paradigm of thought built on a fear of God. Man must accept that he has both a divine and physical nature. These two natures need not war with each other as if one were good and the other evil. In fact, until we complete our journey of redemption and return to the Paradise of Eden, we need to better understand how to successfully marry these two natures. Until man achieves balance and harmony between his divine and physical natures he will remain a citizen of two worlds, yet at home in neither.

Dare We Shatter the Paradigm of Fear?

It is now time for man to shatter the paradigm of fear that has for so long hindered his relationship with God. We must stop being imprisoned by the concept of a God so unloving and a sin so great that it was necessary for the Son of God to offer himself as a human sacrifice in order to give man any hope of reconciliation with God. Even the wonder that is the story of the life of Jesus Christ has been restrained by those same forces of fear and control that have tenaciously endured throughout history. Jesus offered no commandments, no precepts, and no dogma. He founded no religious sect and formed no religious institution. On the contrary, he challenged the established religious institutions and their elevation of the politics and economics of religion over the substance of man's relationship with God. It was his challenge to the established order, and not the message of love that he preached, that resulted in his death.

The message taught by Jesus was simple. It was to love one another. "Therefore all things whatsoever ye would that men should do to you, do ye even so to them" (Matthew 7:12; Luke 6:31). Jesus was to have been the catalyst to usher in a new paradigm built not upon fear, but upon love. The message of Jesus was that the path back to Eden was through the good that flows from love conquering the evil that is the hallmark of the insatiable and selfish desires of man.

And is it not outrageously parochial for man to believe that the Supreme Being we call God would send his Son to our speck of sand to be put to death as a sacrificial lamb for the sins of mankind? Was

God really complicit in such a horrifically horrendous act? Do not Adam and Eve's eating of the forbidden fruit pale by comparison to such an act? Are we really to believe that God exiles man from the Paradise of Eden for an act of disobedience yet allows man, while in exile, to carry out the murder of his Son as a way of providing man with a path to redemption? There is an outrageous incongruity in such a proposition.

We misunderstand the life of Jesus Christ when we contend that he came into the world as the sacrificial lamb to be offered up for the sins of mankind. Jesus was a Teacher of the Way. His life was intended to serve as a model, a beacon of light pointing the way back home to Eden. The death of Jesus was not in payment for the sins of man, but merely the result of the same violent and intolerant forces we have witnessed throughout man's history. Two thousand years after the message of love given to us by Jesus, we are still a world engaged in war and violence. That is because long ago man figured out that one of the best ways to sustain power and control over others was through the use of fear, and what greater fear is there than the fear of God?

It is time for man to get off of this treadmill of fear. To stop being imprisoned by the concept of a sin so great that the death of Jesus Christ was required to give us any hope of a loving God receiving us back into the fold. Let's clearly understand that the only evil in the world is that created by man and inflicted by man upon man. All that is necessary for man's redemption is for man to choose to stop sinning, to choose the good of love over the evil of self-interest.

The Politics of Religion

The reason we fear God is because we do not feel that we have a personal relationship with God. We just do not feel that we know God. We tend to view God as being up there in some far away and inaccessible kingdom. And like Santa, we believe that God is keeping a list of who has been good and who has been evil and that when we die we will receive the appropriate rewards or punishments. Our lack of a truly personal relationship with God has in part been hindered by institutionalized religion, which has made itself the designated intermediary to stand between man and God. The faithful are indoctrinated not to challenge the intermediary role of religious institutions, but instead to accept a program of rules and precepts that the various religious institutions declare have been given by God.

So, with such a divinely inspired program, why does man so dreadfully fear death and his eventual meeting with God? Should not death, as the anticipated reunion with God, be met with the greatest anticipation and joy? Having for so long been told that, although children of God, we are nevertheless sinners and accordingly must be judged as such has framed our anticipated meeting with God.

It is evident that religious institutions do fulfill a most useful purpose. They provide man with a comprehensive program for a devout worship of God and a code of conduct that, if adhered to faithfully, will allow the sincere to live in harmony with their fellow man.

However, providing rituals of worship and rules of behavior and claiming the exclusive authority to speak for God are two very different matters. The time has come to reassess the role of institutional religion in our lives. More importantly, the time has come for each of us to cultivate our own direct and personal relationship with God.

Although it was not Jesus's intention to malign the religious institutions of his day, he nevertheless railed against the politicization of religion and the elevation of rules and regulations to the detriment of man's relationship with God. I also do not wish to denigrate the role played by religious institutions. The various historical religions have proven invaluable in guiding personal conduct and in providing a wholesome environment for the coming together of like-minded individuals. However, since the time of Jesus, history has shown that the politicization of religion, the competition that it generates and the barrier it places between man and his relationship with God continues.

Although Jesus established no religious institution, we nevertheless witness the formation of a religion based upon his birth, life and teachings. The formation of this new religion was sponsored by the Roman Emperor Constantine who was motivated more by political expediency than by any deep religious conviction. He was greatly concerned over the economic impact that the various warring religious factions were causing within his empire. In an effort to maintain peace among these factions, in 325 AD Constantine called together a council of bishops. It was Constantine's hope that in such a gathering the competing religious sects could come to a theological consensus. Although over eighteen hundred bishops from the various religious sects were summoned, only a very small fraction actually attended. Nevertheless, this gathering of bishops was called the Council of Nicæa, and the theological consensus that they reached came to be known as the Nicene Creed. Among the many doctrines adopted, the Nicene Creed declared that there can be but only one holy catholic and apostolic church founded upon the life and teachings of Jesus Christ. Eventually, through the sponsorship of the political forces of Rome, that one holy catholic and apostolic church became known as the Roman Catholic Church.

After the political formation of the Roman Catholic Church efforts to violently eradicate other religious belief systems deemed heretical and contrary to the dogma and cannons of faith adopted at Nicæa were undertaken. Numerous religious Inquisitions were sanctioned by the political hierarchy of the Church. The cruelty and bloodletting of these Inquisitions were a determined effort to find and weed out so-called Christian heretics or those who did not adhere to the orthodox views of the Roman Catholic Church. The Inquisitions lasted for centuries (1184-1834) and resulted in the death of thousands of innocents. The greater purpose of the Inquisitions was to instill fear in the population at large, "… for punishment does not take place primarily and per se for the correction and good of the person punished, but for the public good in order that others may become terrified and weaned away from the evils they would commit." (Nicolas Eymerich, *Directorium Inquisitorum*, 1578 edition, Book 3, p. 137.)

The Inquisitions were not the only method adopted to stamp out perceived heretical belief systems. There were the religious Crusades—a series of military campaigns also sanctioned by the Church. The Crusades were waged primarily against non-Christian religious sects across Europe and the Middle East. The religious Crusades also lasted for centuries (1095-1291) and resulted in the deaths of tens of thousands of innocents, all in the name of God. Yet, is there any tolerance for such violent practices to be found in the life and teachings of Jesus Christ? Did Jesus teach us that it was justified to persecute another child of God because of their personal religious beliefs? Was there ever a time when such practices were sanctioned or condoned by God, the Creator of us all? The answer to all of these questions is an unequivocal no. These many acts of violence sanctioned and condoned by the Roman Catholic Church were for the purpose of creating a paradigm of fear to ensure its political and religious domination and control. However, the Roman Catholic Church was certainly not alone in carrying out such violent practices. History shows us that other religious sects have also engaged in similar violent practices, and for the very same reasons.

Even in modern, and what we consider enlightened times, we too often witness the painful personal, political, and social consequences arising out of religious intolerance and extremism. Oftentimes a failure to adhere to the pronouncement of rules and precepts adopted by a religious sect will carry unpleasant consequences. The severity of the breach of conduct will determine the severity of the penance or punishment to be meted out to the faltering adherent. To this day, in some religious sects marriage outside of one's faith is frowned upon, and in some instances outright forbidden. In some cases, a violation of the religious creed can be so unforgivable as to warrant not only expulsion from the religious body, but disownment by one's own family. And, unfortunately, in some cases a perceived violation of one's religious creed can lead to acts of extreme violence—all in the name of God.

It was this same propensity for religious extremism and the elevation of rules and regulations over an emphasis of man's relationship with God that Jesus condemned. As then the religions of the world today are more like political and economic institutions determined to secure and preserve their market share of the faithful. What better means to ensure institutional viability than through sermons declaring that other belief systems are not of the one true religion, or that adoption of a particular social or political view is anathema to the word of God?

As disturbing as religious intolerance is, so also has the historical treatment of women by various religious sects been. Some of the religions of the world have subtly, if not overtly, contributed to the marginalization of the role and status of women. In some religious sects it is only men who are considered worthy to preach the word of God. The clear implication is that women are unworthy, if not spiritually unclean, and therefore cannot be allowed to serve as messengers of God. Since the expulsion of Adam and Eve from Eden, women have been subjected to the domination of man—a domination that has sought to keep them in subservient and oftentimes demeaning roles.

It is recorded in Genesis that "...she took of the fruit thereof, and did eat, and gave also unto her husband ... and he did eat" (Genesis 3:6). Clearly the emphasis is on the belief that, but for Eve's disobedience of the command of God not to eat of the forbidden fruit, man would still reside in the Paradise of Eden. The complicity of Adam is conveniently overlooked. As a result of the perceived role of Eve in the fall of humanity, women have universally been minimized and often made the subject of degradation and abuse. The atrocities that have been and are still allowed to be inflicted upon women--who are not only the divine and equal counterpart of man, but who are also children of God--is a sin of such magnitude that there is no comparison.

Even if we hold to a belief that it was Eve who initiated this act of disobedience, should we give Adam a pass on his complicity in also disobeying God? Let us not forget that Adam came first and walked within Eden before Eve arrived. We can presume that he was familiar with the various trees in Eden. When Eve handed him the fruit from the Tree of Knowledge, he must have recognized it as the fruit that God had commanded that he not eat. Nevertheless, he chose to do that which God had commanded that he not do. And after he had consumed the forbidden fruit and heard God demanding to know what had happened, Adam, acting cowardly, threw Eve under the rushing train of God's anger saying "…The woman whom thou gavest to be with me, she gave me of the tree, and I did eat" (Genesis 3:12).

Ever since that fateful moment when Adam betrayed the love of Eve, his divine counterpart, the role of women has been marginalized. Yet it is women who are the vehicles of creation. It is women who provide the doorway between the worlds of spirit and matter. It is a testament to the enduring strength and courage of women that man, prone to violence and war, has survived. It has been women, the recipients of unrelenting mistreatment throughout the ages, who have nevertheless sought to temper man's cruelty with love. It is women who foster the development of the divine within mortal man.

Since the expulsion from Eden men have divorced themselves from the feminine within their own divine nature. Man has been running in fear of reuniting with his divine feminine counterpart. Until man learns once again to surrender and unite with what is an indispensable part of his divine nature, he will struggle with his treatment of women, more out of fear than anger. Until men embrace women as the equal and divine partners they have always been the doorway to Eden will remain closed.

It Is All About Choice

Millions of eloquent words have been written by philosophers and theologians about man's divine origin, his temporal existence, and the relationship between the two. We do live in two worlds, one of spirit and one of matter. However, there is little indication that we truly comprehend the nature, relationship, and unity between these two worlds and our place within each.

In the creation story of Genesis we are told that man was created by a supreme being identified as God. However, the creation story ultimately leaves us with a number of questions to which there seem to be no apparent answers. For instance, what measure of love are we to attribute to a God capable of experiencing anger so powerful that he exiles his children from their paradise home into a foreign world of pain and sorrow? And, more importantly, why does it appear that God does so without also giving man any path for reconciliation and a return to paradise? Perhaps the relevant question should be why does man believe this Supreme Being we call God to be capable of experiencing anger?

We must come to understand that God did not banish Adam and Eve from Eden. The dynamics of the divine creation process are beyond mortal man's present comprehension. Man has yet to truly appreciate that God, as the source and wellspring of unconditional love, would not and could not desire to punish or banish any aspect of himself. Although it is true that we do not currently enjoy the Paradise of Eden, this is not due to the decree of God. It is simply the result of choices made. The freedom to choose carries with it a responsibility to act wisely, as our actions carry inevitable consequences. Choices made out of love lead to good consequences. Choices made out of self-desire lead to bad or evil consequences. Those of us who have lost the enjoyment of Eden did so simply because we chose to act out of self-desire instead of love.

Regrettably, throughout the long march of humanity, man has continued to make unwise choices, perpetuating an endless cycle of painful and unpleasant consequences. We should recognize that God, like any parent, anguishes over the mistakes of his children, while at the same time knowing that mistakes carry their own inescapable consequences. If a child gets sick from eating too much, the parent helps the child recover without also imposing consequences—the resulting sickness is the child's inescapable consequence. It is the responsibility of the child to learn when the proper amount of food has been eaten to avoid becoming sick. If we can agree on that basic premise, then we can all benefit from a further inquiry into why man has failed to successfully merge his divine nature with his physical nature to create, befitting his station as a child of God, heaven on earth and a path back to Eden.

However, for those of us who have fallen, getting from here to there requires us to be tested by the challenges arising out of our consumption of the forbidden fruit of the Tree of Knowledge. The challenges presented are nothing more than the struggle between good and evil, between love and self-desire. It was a decision to consume the fruit of the Tree of Knowledge, thereby choosing self-desire over love that has placed this challenge before us. Having made that regretful decision, it now falls upon each of us to wisely choose love over self-desire, good over evil. Only when all of our actions are guided by love will we have redeemed ourselves and be worthy to return to the Paradise of Eden.

The Need to Break Out of the Box

As we continue on our journey, it will be necessary for each of us to open our minds, to think, to question, and to look at this temporal life experience from a perspective unquestionably at odds with current social, political, and religious dogmas. Humanity is at a crossroads. There needs to be a realization that the old paradigm of thought has proven inadequate in providing man with a road map to redemption or of awakening within his heart the realization that he is, has been, and always will be a child of a loving and compassionate God. A new paradigm of thought is necessary if humanity is not only to survive and flourish within this temporal world reality, but also to redeem his fallen yet immortal soul.

PART II

The Story of Creation

More Questions Than Answers

For millennia, the sacred writings of the Old and New Testaments have formed the foundation of man's understanding, not only of his origin, but more importantly, of his relationship with God. There are many who believe that these sacred writings, if not the actual transmitted word of God, are at least words divinely inspired. The greater truth is that these sacred writings comprise a series of allegorical accounts of transcendent and cosmic events, only partially remembered, as they have been passed down from generation to generation. In light of man's ever-expanding conscious awareness, we now have the opportunity to bring greater clarity to those transcendent and cosmic events.

We can readily acknowledge that there are threads of truth in all of the sacred texts of the world. However, even when taken together these threads are insufficient to weave the complete tapestry of the story of man's origin and his relationship with God. This has led to many attempts on the part of man--sometimes well-intended, sometimes not—to supply the missing threads. Even more regrettably, alterations of sacred texts have occurred throughout history at the hand of the political and religious forces of the day as but one means of exercising control over man. Such treatment of the sacred writings inevitably leads to a distortion of the sacred truths that they otherwise reveal.

Likewise, any oral account of an event will lose its literal integrity the more often the account is transmitted. This is all the more certain when succeeding cultures, some very different from the originating culture, seek to convert such accounts into their own very different language. A single word can mean different things among different cultures. There has been less than universal agreement on the translation of ancient Hebrew, Aramaic, and Greek texts, which in part were fashioned out of prior translations of ancient cuneiform writings and oral traditions. As a result, such varied accounts fail to bridge the transcendent and temporal realities particularly when future generations must theorize over what a specific word or symbol was intended to mean or to represent. It is in the Book of Genesis, the first book of the Hebrew Bible, where the story of man's creation is told. However, despite the passage of time, the creation story has proven beyond man's intellectual and moral capacity to fully comprehend. After many centuries, man continues to struggle for that insightful understanding of his creation and more importantly, of his relationship with God.

In Genesis, we learn that man was not just one among the many of God's numerous creations. Man was unique in that he was created in the image and after the likeness of God himself. This apparent favored status was further demonstrated when God endowed man with physical immortality and gave him dominion over all other living things within a paradise garden called Eden. However, at some point after man is elevated to the role of caretaker of Eden, and for a transgression the true nature of which is not clearly explained, an angry God expels man from the Garden of Eden. And it was not just an expulsion. There were also a series of punishments imposed upon the transgressors in Eden.

First, God declares to the woman Eve, "I will greatly multiply thy sorrow and thy conception; in sorrow thou shalt bring forth children" (Genesis 3:16). To "greatly multiply" is to assure a quantity or measure of that which is being multiplied. "Sorrow" can be defined as distress caused by affliction or pain. "Conception" can be defined as the origin or beginning of something conceived such as an idea, a design, or a plan. However, it can also be defined as the inception of pregnancy leading to child bearing. God's punishment upon Eve raises a very interesting point for consideration. It implies that prior to being expelled from the Garden of Eden, Eve did not experience sorrow and that her acts of conception did not produce children. Sorrow and child bearing were direct consequences of Eve's eating the fruit from the tree that God had commanded her not to eat.

And as for Adam, God decrees, "Because thou hast hearkened unto the voice of thy wife, and hast eaten of the tree, of which I commanded thee, saying, 'Thou shalt not eat of it;' cursed is the ground for thy sake; in sorrow shalt thou eat of it [the forbidden fruit] all the days of thy life" (Genesis 3:17). Apparently Adam and Eve cannot un-ring the bell. Having once disobeyed God by eating the fruit of the forbidden tree they will thereafter not only be required to always eat of it, but to do so in a state of sorrow. Instead of enjoying eternal life in paradise, Adam and Eve are condemned to live a life of pain and suffering in a most inhospitable world. Even more disheartening, the creation story offers no apparent avenue for man's rehabilitation or possible return to Eden. It is evident that man is left to discover on his own how, if at all possible, to reconcile and heal his relationship with God.

Man's failure to recognize the deeper spiritual truth hidden in the creation story has led to the concept of God as an entity reflecting the image and likeness of mortal man. In Genesis God is made to appear as a powerful and angry ruler who has no tolerance for those who break his rules. This is the model that man readily adopts as, after all, wasn't man created in the "image and after the likeness of God?" Man's personification of God has too often been the justification for waging war and otherwise brutalizing one another. Unfortunately, the personification of God has distracted man from understanding the true nature of God and of his relationship with God. It has also fed man's ego to the point that he shamelessly claims the authority to speak for God. There is just something so childish in those who declare to know the will of God as relates to the conduct of human affairs.

It is true that man was indeed created in the image and after the likeness of God. However, that image and likeness is not to be found in the form of the physical body. God does not have two arms, two legs, and a head. Unlike man, God is not a person. God is an ineffable power and presence. That image and likeness of God, which in Genesis is named man, is but a reflection of the greater Consciousness of God. That reflection, that image and likeness named man is the Atom of God Consciousness. We should understand that, as a drop of water is to the ocean, so all men, all Atoms of God Consciousness are in their relationship to God. We each are inseparably and eternally united one to each other and all to God.

Admittedly, questions of man's origin and his relationship to God, unlike mathematical equations, cannot be answered with absolute precision, and least of all with absolute certainty. Despite incredible intellectual and technological advancements, man still struggles to achieve an understanding of himself, let alone of the universe in which he lives. The reach of man's mind is still so limited that the mainstream scientific community believes that the small blue rock we call planet Earth, on the outer reaches of a vast galaxy, in a universe of incomprehensible scale and dimension, is the only likely place where human life as we know it exists. Unfortunately, such thinking follows in the traditions that once held that the Earth was not only flat, but also the center of this infinite universe. It is time for man to move beyond the premise that "seeing is believing" to simply believing.

Man Fails to Recognize His Own Divinity

The primary reason man has given too literal an interpretation to the story of creation is because of his inability to recognize his own divine nature. It is truly a case of being unable to see the forest for the trees. We are so fixated on the physical life experience that we fail to see that this temporal material reality is simultaneously bonded to a transcendent spirit reality. And it is precisely because of that failure that a literal interpretation of Genesis leaves us with too many unanswered questions.

For example, if Genesis is a literal account of creation, then what are we to assume has happened to the Garden of Eden? It is evident that it still exists, as Genesis tells us that God "…drove out the man [of Eden]; and he placed at the east gate of the garden of Eden Cherubim, and a flaming sword that turned every way, to keep the way of the tree of life" (Genesis 3:24). What are we to understand is meant by "to keep the way of the tree of life?" In Genesis, we are told that, when eaten, the fruit of the tree of life gives man eternal life. Is it the eternal life within the Garden of Eden that is being preserved against the possible contamination by those who have consumed the forbidden fruit, to keep the cycles of death out of the Garden of Eden?

We know this garden paradise still exists, so whom may we assume has replaced man "to dress it and keep it" (Genesis 2:15)? And why has man been unable to locate it? Many have looked. Some believe Genesis tells us the Garden of Eden was located somewhere in the Middle East, perhaps in Iraq or Turkey. But if that were so, why has man been unable to locate or find any evidence of it? There are others who believe that the Garden of Eden does exist on Earth; just hidden from man's view by the blinding light cast from the Cherubim's flaming sword.

Our creation story, like a favorite fairy tale, starts off with "In the beginning..." Was time the first thing God created? We learn that after creating the heaven and the earth, and a variety of plant and animal life, God then decreed, "Let us make man in our image and after our likeness" (Genesis 1:24). Unfortunately we are not given any indication of exactly what that image and likeness is, other than that "God created he him; male and female created he them" (Genesis 1:27). Does this statement imply that God created man as an androgynous being having both male and female characteristics? If so, how may we envision the nature of and interaction between those bonded male and female characteristics particularly as to God's directive to the man made in his image, to be fruitful and multiply? We are left to surmise whether man, created in the image and likeness of God, was created as a man of spirit only or whether God's image and likeness was also impressed within a material form.

After God creates man he then gives man dominion "...over the earth and every living thing that moveth upon the earth" (Genesis 1:28). Clearly, God did place man at the pinnacle of creation. Yet confusion arises when, after having created man and vesting him with authority over all living things, we are then told "God formed man [of] the dust of the ground, and breathed into his nostrils the breath of life, and man became a living soul" (Genesis 2:7). What are we to make of this second act of creation? How are we to view the man created in the image and after the likeness of God from the man formed of the dust of the ground?

The story goes on to tell us that God put the man he had formed into a paradise garden located in a placed called Eden. In this Garden of Eden were planted two special fruit-bearing trees. One of the trees is called the Tree of Life. We are told that when eaten, the fruit of the Tree of Life would give man eternal life. The implication being that so long as man ate of the Tree of Life his physical body formed of the dust of the ground would remain imperishable and never die. The other tree is called the Tree of Knowledge of good and evil. We are not told how this Tree of Knowledge can be both good and evil at the same time. Or why eating the fruit of this tree would cause man to die, "…thou shalt not eat of it: for in the day that thou eatest thereof thou shalt surely die" (Genesis 2:17). We know from our story that after eating the fruit of the Tree of Knowledge, Adam and Eve did not immediately die, at least not in a literal sense. Death came only much later, and only after their expulsion from Eden. So what manner of death is implied from eating the fruit of the Tree of Knowledge? If not immediate and literal then perhaps it is an allegorical form of death symbolic of a loss of eternal life, of immortality. Whether it is a literal or allegorical form of death, we are left to speculate why God put such a dangerous tree in the paradise he had created for man. Or whether perhaps eating the fruit of the Tree of Knowledge was dangerous and evil only when consumed by man, but was good when eaten by every other living thing within the Garden of Eden.

Moving on, our story tells us "…God said, [It is] not good that the man should be alone; I will make him a[n] help meet for him" (Genesis 2:18). Are we to assume that God did not plan ahead when he created Adam? And what are we to understand is meant when God declares he will make Adam a "helper?" Are we seeing the stage being set to place woman in a subservient role to the needs of man?

It is also interesting that when it came to the creation of Eve, God went in a totally different direction. After having formed Adam out of the dust of the ground, God puts Adam into a deep sleep and removes one of his ribs. It is with the rib from Adam that God fashions the body of Eve. Why did God not create Eve in the same manner that he had created Adam? Are we to discern any significance in the manner in which the body of Adam was formed from the manner in which the body of Eve was formed? Can we nevertheless assume that Eve also embodied the image and the likeness of God? Certainly such thoughtful considerations of the creation of Eve present a somewhat confusing picture. Should we look upon Adam as the mother and/or father or perhaps the brother of Eve? In any event, the account of the creation of Eve suggests she enjoys a somewhat subservient status in that she owes her existence as much to the man Adam as to God.

As we continue with our story we are introduced to the "serpent" of the Garden of Eden. We are told that this serpent was "more subtil than any beast of the field which the Lord God had made"

(Genesis 3:1) A serpent is often portrayed as a symbol representing cunning and deceit. And as we learn such was not only the character of this serpent, but that this serpent also possessed the capacity to walk among, and to talk with, Adam and Eve. We are left to wonder what image and likeness this serpent was modeled after, and why God would create someone or something having the capacity to challenge his established order within paradise. We also struggle to understand why God would place before Adam and Eve such dangers as that of a deadly fruit and a cunning intelligence in the idyllic paradise home he had created for them?

As our story unfolds, we learn that Adam and Eve were persuaded by the serpent to eat the fruit of the Tree of Knowledge, the fruit that God had commanded they not eat. After committing this act of disobedience, Adam and Eve "...heard the voice of the LORD God walking in the garden...and ...[they] hid themselves...amongst the trees of the garden" (Genesis 3:8). God called out to Adam and said, "...Where [art] thou?" (Genesis 3:9). Eventually, Adam comes out of hiding and has a conversation with God, a conversation to which Eve no doubt took exception. Adam tells God that "...The woman whom thou gavest [to be] with me, [is this where the treatment of woman as property began?], she gave me of the tree, and I did eat" (Genesis 3:12). Obviously, this conversation does not speak highly of Adam as he attempts to throw all of the blame onto Eve.

We learn that after having consumed the forbidden fruit, things go very badly for Adam and Eve. They are evicted from the Garden of Eden because as proclaimed by God, "Behold, the man is become as one of us, to know good and evil..." (Genesis 3:22). Are we to assume that God or the Gods of the "one of us" ate freely the fruit of the Tree of Knowledge? What was it about the fruit of the Tree of Knowledge that God did not wish to share with Adam and Eve? Why would God not want his children, Adam and Eve, to become "as one of us"? Are we to infer that something significant is to be gained when combining the fruit from the Tree of Life with the fruit of Tree of Knowledge?

Perhaps what is being narrated in Genesis are but partial truths surrounding the cosmological beginnings of man that the authors of Genesis were ill-equipped to understand and therefore to correctly report upon. When we talk to our young children we often tell a story to convey a larger more important message. In like manner,

Jesus often spoke to his disciples in parables. Yet, oftentimes Jesus, after telling one of his parables, found it necessary to chastise his disciples for placing too literal an interpretation on a story that was in fact intended to convey a cosmic truth. Collectively man has demonstrated an inability to see the creation story as a bridge to greater transcendent truths.

Despite the intellectual heights reached in his long evolutionary march, man still looks at the story of creation in a childlike way. Do we really believe that the profound reality that is God, and of man's creation and his relationship to God, can fully and adequately be explained within the few pages of Genesis? Do we really believe that within those few pages, we find an accurate portrayal of God and his relationship with man? In creating man in his own image and likeness, God demonstrated man's elevated status among the many created. Yet, God also plants a tree in the garden paradise of Eden the fruit of which if eaten is deadly, at least deadly if eaten by man. True enough, man is told not to eat the deadly fruit, but God does not tell man why eating the fruit of this particular tree will cause him to "surely die." Nor is there any commentary as to the intended purpose for such a deadly tree being in this paradise garden. Was the fruit of this tree intended to be eaten by someone other than man? Furthermore, it is not just a tree dangerous to Adam and Eve that God puts in this paradise garden. God also places a serpent in the garden having apparent and commanding powers of persuasion. And when Adam and Eve are persuaded by the serpent to eat the forbidden fruit, it is not enough that God takes away their immortality and exiles them from Eden. He also decrees that said punishment shall fall upon all of their generations to follow. In other words, the innocent shall nevertheless, all be born clothed in the sin of Adam and Eve and required to suffer the same consequences.

The story of creation does not give man any apparent hope that he may ever be allowed to return to Eden. There is no discernible path offered to man for his redemption or reconciliation with God. Instead God declares to Adam, "...for dust thou [art] and unto dust shalt thou return" (Genesis 3:19). Regrettably, Genesis, when taken literally is, at best, a poorly written and, at worst, a contradictory account of the most significant event known to man—his own creation. When read as a literal account, it raises more questions than it provides answers. Whether authored by the mind of man or inspired by the mind of God, Genesis is a document best understood when read and treated as an allegorical story of a cosmological and transcendent event.

Genesis – The Story of Creation Revealed in Two Acts

When read as an allegorical account, Genesis is deeply rich in meaning and truth. In Genesis, we are presented with several creative events occurring within two separate and distinct acts of creation. In Act I of Genesis, we learn of the formation of the heaven and the earth as a transcendent world of spirit not yet clothed with the substance of matter. In Act II, we learn of the clothing of the heaven and the earth with physical matter and its emergence as the cosmological paradise of Eden.

Genesis Act I

God As Precedent

In Act I of Genesis, we are told, "In the beginning God created the heaven and the earth" (Genesis 1:1), "And the earth was without form, and void…and darkness was upon the face of the deep. And the Spirit of God moved upon the face of the waters (Genesis 1:2). In this introduction, we are introduced to the story's main character identified as God. We are not told that God was himself created, so it is reasonable to assume that there was no precedent to God. Simply stated, God is an inexpressible and inexplicable power, an eternal presence without beginning or end. Accordingly, God cannot be contained within a descriptive name, as one cannot describe that which has no precedent. It is only that which emerges out of this ineffable power called God that can be named.

The introduction also reveals the theme of the story, which is creation. We are told that in the beginning God created. We may therefore reasonably assume that prior to the beginning of creation God was inactive and at rest, as a reality only unto himself. Likewise, the stage of the creation story is set when we are told that "in the beginning God created the heaven and the earth, and the earth was without form, and void." This introductory characterization of the earth is certainly compatible with the use of the word "beginning," which implies the commencement of something and not the completion of something. However, the use of the term "earth" does raise questions. Is Genesis referring to that tiny blue rock floating within the boundless expanse of the universe that we call the planet Earth? If so, are there then other creation stories for all of the other tiny rocks and grains of sand also floating within the infinite expanse of the universe?

And how are we to envision the earth of Genesis, whether it is just a planet or something altogether different, as existing yet "without form, and void"? Is Genesis telling us that creation occurs first through an activity akin to thought occurring within the Consciousness of God and that only later will the thoughts or Spirit of God take on form and substance? Unlike the earth, our introduction does not mention whether in the beginning the heaven was also void and without form. The word heaven does imply an essence of spirit as opposed to matter. For our present orientation, we may presume that spirit always precedes both form and matter and that, in the beginning, both the heaven and the earth were created transcendently as spirit, void and without form.

In the introduction, we are further introduced to the "face of the deep" and the "face of the waters". First, we are told that darkness [was] upon the face of the deep. What are we to make of this cryptic statement? We know that the word deep is often used to describe the depth of a body of water or the vastness of space. We are also told that the Spirit of God moved upon the face of the waters. Is it reasonable to assume that these two faces refer to the same one reality? Whether the same or not, the face of the deep and the face of the waters would appear to be pre-existing realities, as Genesis does not report that God created the deep or the waters. Therefore, I will suggest that the face of the deep and the face of the waters refer to that pre-existing ineffable all-encompassing power and eternal presence identified in Genesis as God.

The Spirit of God

What understanding should we draw from the introduction's reference to the Spirit of God? We have concluded that as a pre-existing, ineffable, and all-encompassing power, there is nothing greater than God. Perhaps the Spirit of God simply refers to a characteristic, a quality, or essence of God. However, God, having no precedent, is incapable of being described or qualified, as to do so would impose a limitation of that which is being so qualified or described. God just is. And although we use such words such as omnipresent, omnipotent, and omniscience to describe God, we do so in a human effort to mentally grasp the ineffable; that which cannot otherwise be grasped or understood.

This Spirit [of God] can be viewed as the characterization of an activity occurring within the mind of God or what I will refer to as the waters of the infinite Consciousness of God. It is only after we are told that the Spirit of God "moved" upon the face of the waters that the individual acts of creation commenced. Movement can be defined as a change from one state to another. As previously stated, God just is—an incomprehensible power that, in the absence of an act of creation, is inactive and at rest. It is the movement of the Spirit of God that precedes the acts of creation. The Spirit of God is the active power that leads to creation. We cannot know what occurred within the ineffable power called God to cause the Spirit of God to be stirred into action. Although we may assume that this movement did not affect any change in the ineffable power we call God, it did, however, result in something amazing emerging within the Consciousness of God.

Perhaps this movement of the Spirit of God can be likened to the sound and oscillating movement of a beating heart. And, once awakened from his state of quiet solitude by this sound and movement, God was then moved to perpetually experience the rhythmic beat of his own heart, a movement that gave birth to a creative impulse that will never end. All is God; all emanates out of God and all the limitless heartbeats of creation will remain within the body of God. Clearly it was the movement of this creative force identified as the Spirit of God that was the initiating cause leading to those evolutionary stages of greater diversity and complexity and that Genesis describes overall as creation. We can also view the movement of the

Spirit of God as sound, the sound of the Spoken Word of God. After all, creation only occurs after God first says, "Let there be...."

Emergence Within the Precedent

In Act I of Genesis it is implied that the first thing God created was the heaven and the earth. However, the first thing God created was "light." And God said, "Let there be light, and there was light" (Genesis 1:3). "And God divided the light from the darkness" (Genesis 1:4). It is clear that darkness was an existing state or condition of the face of the deep as we are told that darkness [was] upon the face of the deep. How may we view this darkness reflected in the face of the deep? Clearly darkness denotes an absence of light. I would go further and suggest that it also implies a state of silent stillness as in a state of deep rest or sleep. However we may choose to look at the darkness it is clear that the status quo of the darkness was altered when the Spirit of God moved upon the face of the waters creating light.

The movement of the Spirit of God upon the face of the waters can be seen as a catalytic activity igniting a reaction within the quiet stillness of the waters; a reaction of such intensification that it led to the creation of light. "And God divided the light from the darkness" (Genesis 1:4). Light now emerges from within the waters as an opposing force or power to darkness. However we may choose to view the creation of light, it is obvious that the light has coequal standing with the darkness, as "God divided the light from the darkness and called the light Day and the darkness Night" (Genesis 1:5).

It is only after creating light as the companion of darkness that God then creates the heaven. "And God said let there be a firmament in the midst of the waters, and let it divide the waters from the waters" (Genesis 1:6). "And God called the firmament Heaven" (Genesis 1:8). It is apparent that the waters, now containing the coequal powers or forces of light and darkness, are the source from out of which will be drawn not only the heaven but also the earth. All flows out of the waters that are the infinite Consciousness of God, now to be given form by the push and pull of the interactive union between light and darkness. It is light through its interaction with darkness that gives birth to light that is illuminating. This illuminating light, which is neither all light nor all darkness, is the substance born out of the interactive union between light and darkness. This illuminating light, which we can also identify as the illuminating light of consciousness as it emanates from out of the infinite Consciousness of God, is the malleable substance that will now be used to clothe all those evolutionary stages of greater complexity emerging out of the waters and that Genesis describes overall as creation.

The waters represent a primordial reality greater than all that emerges out of it. It is a reality greater than that of either the light or the darkness, which are mere attributes; greater than that of the combined union of light and darkness; greater than that of the heaven and the earth; and greater than all that will later materialize and evolve out of the heaven and the earth. The waters represent the infinite Consciousness of God—that vast and unbounded reality from and out of which all else emerges.

We can never know what triggered the movement of the Spirit of God within the Consciousness of God. Nevertheless, we may perceive of this movement as the initiating cause of the event that Science refers to as the Big Bang and that religion calls creation. Once so initiated—once set in motion by this catalytic activity of the Spirit of God—creation would continue to manifest and unfold in greater and greater diversity and complexity through the endless interactive union between the power of light and the power of darkness. All creation first emerges out of the Consciousness of God as spirit moving and evolving through a materialization and densification of the light substance born of the union between light and darkness. The continuing process of the materialization and densification of the illuminating light of consciousness eventually leads to the clothing of spirit with matter. This is an evolutionary process whereby the two, spirit and matter, become the one unified reality.

The Evolution of Consciousness
Leads to Spirit Clothed in Matter

It is through the interplay between light and darkness as coequal partners, the light representative of the masculine principle and darkness representative of the feminine principle that the firmament first emerges. The firmament is the envelope—that quantum field in, through and upon which will be impressed, as an exquisite tapestry, all creation emanating out of the waters that are the Consciousness of God. This envelope of the firmament, having emerged from within the Consciousness of God, now exists as a distinct reality, nevertheless within and surrounded by the waters that are the Consciousness of God. We must always remember that all that there is, above and below, is the Consciousness of God. All realities that come into existence are a part of and remain contained within the infinite Consciousness of God.

"And God made the firmament, and divided the waters which [were] under the firmament from the waters which were above the firmament" (Genesis 1:7). We should not be confused by spatial references to the waters above and the waters below, as there are no such spatial realities possible when we talk about the Consciousness of God, or of that which emerges from within it. All is one reality, no matter what its appearance or form. The firmament divides the waters, not in a literal sense, as one cannot divide the unity that is the Consciousness of God. Allegorically, the division of the waters represents the emergence of "the earth" within the all-encompassing firmament; that envelope of illuminating light called "the heaven." The so-called division of the waters occurs within the waters of the firmament, which itself has emerged out of the waters that are the infinite Consciousness of God.

"And the waters below the firmament were gathered together in one place. Out of these waters were drawn dry land called Earth and the gathered waters were called Seas" (Genesis 1:9-10). With the emergence of the earth within the firmament that is the heaven, we see those evolutionary stages of greater complexity arising out of the interactive union between light and darkness. The Earth is a further materialization and densification of that illuminating light of consciousness born of the union between light and darkness. This materialization and densification of the substance, or waters, occurring within the envelope of the firmament is what is meant by the separation of the waters below from the waters above. The earth, which we were told was without form and void, now takes on form, although not yet physical form, as all creation occurring in Act I is clothed in the form and light substance of spirit only. The earth's relationship to the heaven is now made clear as the earth emerges from out of the waters of the firmament, from out of the substance of light, the illuminating light of consciousness.

After the emergence of the Earth out of the waters of the firmament, we see the further evolution of the illuminating light of consciousness with the emergence of the plant realm. "And God said let the earth bring forth grass, the herb yielding seed, [and] the fruit tree" (Genesis 1:11). This was followed with the emergence of "lights" in the heaven. "And God said let there be lights in the firmament of the heaven to divide the day from the night" (Genesis 1:14). With the emergence of the lights, we see the further evolution of the illuminating light of consciousness with the materialization out of the waters of the firmament of the stars and planets, of suns and moons, and the cycles they all bring of day and night. This was followed with the emergence of the animal realm. And finally we are told of the emergence of man created in the image and after the likeness of that ineffable power we call God (Genesis 1:26).

What becomes clear is that each succeeding level of creation emerges out of the preceding level and accordingly is more intricate in development and degrees of consciousness. Man, created as an Atom of God Consciousness and being the last of that which was created in Act I, contains within his divine matrix all that has preceded him in the many evolutionary stages of creation. It is because the divine matrix that is man possesses the highest degree of the evolution of consciousness within creation that he is endowed with dominion over all the earth and over every living thing that moveth upon the earth (Genesis, 1:26, 1:28).

The obvious question is: who or what formed the template, the blueprint, the archetypal design for the variety of form and expression of consciousness within creation? The answer truly is God. All that was, is, or ever will be already exists within the infinite Consciousness of God. There is nothing that can manifest into form that does not already exist in the Consciousness of God. Creation is the manifestation of unlimited multi-dimensional realities of consciousness perpetually unfolding throughout a never-ending eternity. Man, as an Atom of God Consciousness, is one of those incredible realities.

In Act I, God does not name man—only acknowledging that he "…created man in his [own] image, in the image of God created he him; male and female created he them" (Genesis 1:27). It is my contention that the image and likeness of God, which I have chosen to identify as the Atom of God Consciousness, and which in Genesis is called man, is that of an androgynous being having both a masculine and feminine polarity of consciousness. Also, I suggest that "created he them" means God created man as a class or group and not as one "Atom" of God Consciousness. God said unto them, "Be fruitful, and multiply, and replenish the earth, and subdue it; and have dominion over…every living thing that moveth upon the earth" (Genesis 1:28). Some believe that this is a directive to man to propagate—to have children. Perhaps; however, I believe it is a broader directive to each androgynous Atom of God Consciousness to exercise creative dominion over the earth "to be fruitful, and multiply, and replenish the earth, and subdue it" (Genesis 1:28).

We can reasonably infer two propositions from such a broad directive. We know that it was God who created "the earth and every living thing that moveth upon the earth," including man. Therefore, the authority and power granted to man to be fruitful, to multiply, to replenish and subdue the earth would imply that man was also endowed with a power to create. Secondly, having been endowed with such broad authority suggests that man, unlike the varied plant and animal species upon the earth, did not need to be replenished. Man, having been created in the image and after the likeness of God, as an Atom of God Consciousness, was an immortal being.

At the close of Act I, we see the creation of a world of spirit formed but not yet clothed in physical matter. In this first act of creation, the blueprint for all realities emanating within the Infinite Consciousness of God was given 'form' as spirit through a coalescing of the substance of light—the illuminating light of consciousness—brought about through the union between light and darkness. In Act II of Genesis, we will see the further evolution of the world of spirit, of the heaven and the earth, by its being clothed with physical matter.

Genesiss Act II

Man as the Atom of God Consciousness
Takes on Physical Form and Becomes Adam

In Act II of Genesis we learn of the further evolution of the earth and of man. This evolution unfolds throughout the generations by a further coalescing and densification of the illuminating light substance of consciousness. In Act II, we see that the many forms of spirit are now to be dressed in the clothing of physical matter. Act II begins with the declaration that the Lord God made "every plant of the field before it was in the earth, and every herb of the field before it grew; for the Lord God had not caused it to rain upon the earth, and there was not a man to till the ground" (Genesis 2:5). Genesis is here telling us that the heaven and the earth, the sun and stars, the plants and animals, as well as man, were first created as spirit, lacking in physical form.

"But there went up a mist from the earth, and watered the whole face of the ground" (Genesis 2:6), "and the Lord God formed man [of] the dust of the ground, and breathed into his nostrils the breath of life; and man became a living soul" (Genesis 2:7). There is a much revealed for consideration in this short statement. There is the mist from the earth, the face of the ground, and the dust of the ground, the breath of life, and the living soul. Let's start with the mist from the earth. Mist is defined as condensed water vapor. We can view this mist of the waters coming up from the earth as the further coalescing and densification of the waters of the earth, which itself had coalesced out of the waters of the firmament. It is through this further coalescing of the waters, of the substance of the illuminating light of consciousness that the face of the ground, the face of the earth, takes on a physical material form. After the mist has watered the whole face of the earth, the earth is now clothed in the material substance of the illuminating light of consciousness, now further coalesced into and materialized as the face of the ground, as the physical earth. And how may we view the dust of the ground? Dust is described as any material in the form of powder or tiny particles. The dust of the ground of Genesis is composed of tiny particles of light matter resting upon the face of the ground. It is from the lighter dust resting upon the face of the ground that God forms man's physical body.

When Genesis tells us that God formed man of the dust of the ground, we are not being told that God created man a second time. In Act I we see that man was created as spirit man. I have chosen to call this man of spirit the Atom of God Consciousness. This Atom of God Consciousness came into being through the sound of the Spoken Word, the sound of the AT-OM. When spoken AT refers to where man first appears. Man first appears in the OM, or in the sound born of the movement of the Spirit of God within the Consciousness of God. The sound of creation, the sound of the OM, is the sound of the Spoken Word of God. As spirit man, as ATOM, man lacked a physical material body. It is in Act II that we see that God formed man a physical body to clothe his spirit Atom of God Consciousness.

However, God did something more than simply form man a physical body out of the dust of the ground. "And the Lord God formed man [of] the dust of the ground, and breathed into his nostrils the breath of life, and the man became a living soul" (Genesis 2.7) The breath of God is eternal, as there is nothing of God, which is not eternal. It is the energy of the breath of God flowing into the nostrils of man that not only enlivens man's physical material body, but also transforms it into an incorruptible physical body of light. With the breath of God, man now becomes a 'living soul'. Soul does not refer to the spiritual nature of man, to the spirit Atom of God Consciousness. Soul refers to that energetic clothing now worn by each spirit Atom of God Consciousness as a permanent and incorruptible physical body of light.

The spirit Atom of God Consciousness, now clothed with physical matter, is evolved into the physical man Adam. It is the bonding of matter to spirit that allows for the continuing evolution of all Atoms of God Consciousness. In that context, AD refers to the matter that is added or bonded to the spirit Atom of God Consciousness. AM refers to the consciousness of the Atom of God Consciousness now made self-aware as the physical man Adam, an independent self-aware I AM consciousness. It is this I AM consciousness, resident within a permanent and incorruptible physical body of light that makes man so unique within all of creation. There are no other expressions of life within nature that are likewise endowed with the permanent breath of God, a conscious self-awareness or an incorruptible physical body of light. Within all of nature it is only man, now formed as the physical man Adam, who is not subject to the cycles and forces of nature, but who has complete authority over them.

After man received his physical garment, the clothing of the many other spirit forms of creation continued. "And the Lord God planted a garden eastward in Eden, and there he put the man whom he had formed" (Genesis 2:8). "And out of the ground the Lord God formed every beast of the field and every fowl of the air; and brought [them] unto Adam..." (Genesis 2:19). Here the story of creation deepens. We are introduced to a place called Eden. We are not told that God created this place called Eden, only that he planted a garden eastward in Eden. Eden is nothing other than the earth now clothed in physical matter brought about through the densification of the illuminating light of consciousness. The garden planted in Eden refers to the realm of nature and what will be the home to all physical life in Eden, including man.

It is noteworthy that in Act I man was the last to be created, but in Act II he is the first to be formed and dressed with the clothing of physical matter. It is also significant that God formed man's body of the dust of the ground (Genesis 2:7), while forming the bodies of beasts of the field from out of the ground (Genesis 2:19). The physical clothing woven of the dust of the ground, of tiny particles of light, was less coarse and dense than that woven from the material drawn from out of the ground. The physical body of light worn by man was made to be incorruptible and immortal. However, after appropriate cycles, the physical clothing worn by all the other expressions of life within the Garden of Eden was intended to return to the ground from whence it had been taken.

It is after God had planted the Garden in Eden and "…formed every beast of the field" that we now see all the spirit forms of creation identified in Act I dressed in physical matter. We also see the unique standing of man within the Garden of Eden. As a parent would name a child so to God names his child. The spirit Atom of God Consciousness now becomes the physical man, Adam. And as with a favored child, God endows Adam with the authority to not only name every living creature within the Garden in Eden, but to dress it and keep this paradise garden (Genesis 2:15). Now clothed with an immortal soul, an imperishable physical body of light, it is man alone who is given dominion over every living thing within the Garden of Eden.

The Transformation of Adam and the Emergence of Eve

In Act I of Genesis, God declared, "Let us make man in our image, after our likeness" (Genesis 1:26). "So God created man in his [own] image, in the image of God created he him; male and female created he them" (Genesis 1:27). In other words, that image and likeness of God represented in the Atom of God Consciousness is that of an androgynous being having a unified masculine and feminine polarity of consciousness. It is essential to understand that by masculine and feminine we are not talking about the sexes or of the relationship between the sexes. We are talking about the ineffable powers of consciousness resident within the Consciousness of God and therefore, within each individualized Atom of God Consciousness.

It was as the androgynous being of spirit, as the Atom of God Consciousness, that in Act I," man was given dominion over all the earth and over every living thing that moveth upon the earth" (Genesis 1:26, 1:28). However, after the earth and every living thing are clothed with physical matter, man, now as the embodied Adam, is charged "to dress and to keep" the Garden of Eden. This is an expansion of the authority first given man in Act I, and implies that man is now further endowed with the creative authority to dress all living things in nature, with physical matter.

Adam first exercises his creative authority when he names every beast of the field. It was God who named man, Adam. Once named by God, man then stands within nature consciously self-aware as the embodied I AM consciousness. Nothing else within Eden is equal to man. Likewise, in naming the beasts of the field, Adam exercises his creative authority by giving identity to all that God has formed out of the ground. Unlike the voice and breath of God, the lesser voice and breath of Adam cannot endow the beasts of the field with physical immortality. Yet Adam can, with his breath, his Spoken Word, fulfill his authority to exercise dominion over, and to dress, keep, and replenish, all that resides within the paradise Garden of Eden.

After being put in the Garden of Eden, Adam goes through a further and profound transformation. God says "It is not good that the man should be alone; I will make him a help meet for him" (Genesis 2:18). So God took a rib from Adam and made a woman. Here we see the separation of the unified masculine and feminine polarities of consciousness within the androgynous Adam. "Adam called his companion Wo-man, because she was taken out of man" (Genesis 2:23). It is at this point in the creation story that we witness not only the bifurcation or division of the living soul, of the incorruptible physical body of light of Adam, but also of the unified consciousness of Adam. In this act of bifurcation, the feminine polarity of consciousness within the androgynous Adam is now withdrawn to stand independent in a separate yet also incorruptible physical body as the woman Eve.

It is because Eve comes out of Adam that Genesis does not report the creation of Eve as having occurred in the same fashion as that of Adam. However, having been drawn out of Adam, Eve cannot but also reflect the image and likeness of God. There is no question of the greater or the lesser. It is the plan of evolution for each Adam of God Consciousness that the equal and harmonious union between the masculine and feminine polarities of consciousness continues upon the bifurcation of the androgynous Adam. Now as two, Adam and Eve were nevertheless intended to continue to unite as one in consciousness. It is in the union or marriage of their respective polarities of consciousness that the man, Adam, and the woman, Eve, were intended to create, to be fruitful and to multiply.

A deeper reading of Genesis reveals the significance of separating the polarities of consciousness within the androgynous Adam. "Therefore, shall a man leave his father and his mother, and shall cleave unto his wife; and they shall be one flesh" (Genesis 2:24). Here Genesis is telling us a man shall leave his unified androgynous state, his father and his mother, and thereafter the man now as the masculine polarity of consciousness shall cleave unto his wife the woman now as the feminine polarity of consciousness.

However, the statement that the two "shall be one flesh" does not refer to a physical sexual union. The instruction to man to "cleave unto his wife" is a directive to man to be faithful to his bonded union with the feminine polarity of consciousness now resident in a separate physical body. The declaration that "they shall be one flesh" means that both the man and the woman shall preserve the incorruptible nature of their respective yet shared physical bodies of light. In that sense the two "shall be one flesh." A failure in that regard would not only result in a contamination of their respective physical bodies, it would tear asunder the unified nature of their respective polarities of consciousness.

Adam and Eve as immortals would have no need to engage in an act of physical self-propagation. It was not possible through a physical sexual union for Adam and Eve to create other "immortal" physical Adams and Eves. Such power of creation would require the power of the Spoken Word of God. In Genesis 2:25 we are told "And they were both naked, the man and his wife, and were not ashamed." They were not ashamed because their physical bodies did not have sexual organs. They had no purpose within the Garden of Eden for such organs. But then spoke the serpent.

PART III

Genesis Retold

Dare We Look Behind the Veil?

Scientists and theologians both agree that the creation of our universe was precipitated by some phenomenal event. For science this extraordinary causal event is believed to have been an explosion of cosmic proportions. Science has characterized this event as the Big Bang cosmological theory of creation. That which underwent this cosmic explosion is theorized to have been a very small, dense mass of energy and matter. However, the hatching of this cosmic egg remains but a theory, as science has been unable to identify the inherent characteristics of the energy and matter that exploded. Nor, for that matter, has science been able to confirm the existence of any reality, be it of energy or matter, prior to this cosmological explosion. We are therefore left with many questions, the most significant of which is where did this cosmic egg come from?

Some scientists speculate that the cosmic egg may have emerged outside of time and space as we currently understand those states. Maybe it is not a case of looking outside of our dimensional envelope; perhaps time and space are universal conditions that are qualitatively, if not quantitatively, different in realities of consciousness that are presently unknown to man. However, if time and space as we currently understand them exist only in our three-dimensional envelope, then what might a reality absent of time and space look like? Could there possibly be other so-called "dimensional" realities where time and space do exist, but interact differently? If such alternate realities exist, might we expect that energy and matter would retain the same universal characteristics? Perhaps in such alternate realities energy and matter might appear in a form or unity we would not recognize because of our limited understanding of the possible variable interplay between time, space and matter?

For example, would our planet still be recognizable as a spherical planet from a perspective outside of our three-dimensional envelope? Or, could our planet theoretically exist in the absence of time, space, and matter, at least as we currently understand those states? And were it possible to enter such an alternate dimensional reality, would we nevertheless experience consciousness as we now do? And would we recognize our collective presence as 'humanity' or something altogether different? Any attempt to answer such questions would first require serious entertainment of the existence of an alternate reality, or perhaps of other layered realities interwoven with our own three-dimensional reality.

For theologians, the precipitating event that resulted in the creation of the universe was the Spoken Word uttered by a supreme being called God. However, religion has failed to provide man with an embraceable comprehension of God, of an understanding of the creation process, or more importantly, of man's relationship to God. Instead, religion has been content to fall back upon the reliance of faith in the existence of God, and of the unfolding reality that lead to the creation of man and the universe. Yet a reliance on faith alone has not allowed religion to offer any meaningful insight as to why God would choose to place man on but one small rock in a galaxy too large to explore and in a universe too large to comprehend. Furthermore, religion's contention that man lives in a world of pain and suffering because he disobeyed God falls short of bringing greater understanding of the nature of man's 'original sin' and how he may redeem himself of its consequences. After all, it has been a very long time since our exile. Yet the journey home, the journey of redemption, seems to have no ending. To suggest that man need simply accept on faith that the greater wisdom of God is at play amounts to an abandonment of any meaningful search for the fullness of the reality we call God. More importantly, reliance on faith alone has not advanced man's understanding on the profundity of his relationship with God.

Whether one favors the Big Bang or the Spoken Word theory of creation, it is only rational to assume that our universe was 'born' by emerging out of a pre-existent spirit reality wherein time, space, and matter form a unified inseparable state, or out of a material reality wherein time, space, and matter are separate yet interactive states. Whether of spirit or mater, there would, of necessity, have been a pre-existent reality.

Science tells us that all matter is composed of energy. However, energy itself is not matter, but more of a catalyst in the formation of matter. And when matter ceases to be matter and dissolves, there still remains the energy with which it had been bonded. Therefore, we can reasonably conclude that pure energy was the essential primary force that was pre-existent prior to the formation of our material universe. However, how do we get from a pre-existing state of energy to the formation of matter and, more importantly, to the diversity of physical matter within our universe? Are we to believe that physical matter has evolved out of a limitless field of energy as a wholly random occurrence? Are we to assume that a random interaction between neutrons, electrons, and protons can result in the variation of material objects we find within our universe, not the least significant of which is man?

There are those who will argue that we need not assume anything existed before the Big Bang or the Spoken Word, or that, in any event, the magnitude of a search for such a primordial reality is beyond man's present intellectual capacity. However, there are many curious minds that are not the least intimidated by undertaking such an adventure. Let us join with such intellectual explorers confidently, going in search of realities existing outside of our envelope of space, time, and matter—realities that we cannot deny exist, or how could our known envelope exist? We must have the courage to venture out of the intellectual confinement we have fashioned with our physical senses. It is now time for man to awaken his higher senses of consciousness and explore those greater realities of which he truly is the most significant part.

For those of us who believe such bold exploration is not futile, the initial question becomes: how might we perceive this pre-existent primordial state and what might be its characteristics? First, for the purpose of discussion, we may agree that this pre-existent primordial state had no prior precedent and thus avoid the impossible search for the ultimate beginning of the ultimate beginning, ad infinitum. We may also agree that such a pre-existent primordial state exists outside of our experience of time, space, and matter as we currently understand those principles, simply because we have been unable to find the answer to our inquiry within that experience.

Given the apparent infinite scale of the universe, it is reasonable to assume such a pre-existent primordial state would likewise have to be infinite. Also, believing that the creation of the universe began with noise and movement, either from a Big Bang or the Spoken Word, we may, by comparison, presume this pre-existent primordial state to be a state of quiet stillness and as yet unrealized potential. We may further stipulate that our pre-existing primordial state would, of necessity, have to be a non-physical state, as it is the state from and out of which our material envelope of space, time, and matter emerged. It is true that our universe could have originated within a physically larger meta-universe. However, even if that were the case, our inquiry would simply shift to exploring that pre-existent state out of which the meta-universe emerged. Nonetheless, I agreed to simplify our examination of the pertinent question by avoiding the ad infinitum trap.

Therefore, let's summarize the characteristics of this precedent primordial reality as being one of formless energy, having no limits of scale, containing infinite and unlimited potential, and existing within an unbroken silent stillness. The closest analogy we could contemplate of such a primordial reality would be to image our universe existing without any material objects; no planets, stars, or galaxies—just a black and silent void. Even so, such an empty universe would still not equate with our theoretical precedent primordial state, as even a universe empty of all objects would still theoretically contain that energy canvas, that quantum field of energy upon which and within which all of the contents of the universe are suspended. Unlike our theoretical precedent primordial state, even an empty universe would theoretically have the physicality of the substance of space.

So, what can we theorize to be the intrinsic quality or qualities of this precedent primordial pre-existent state? As the heart can never know or comprehend the body of which it is a part, we can acknowledge that we can never truly know or comprehend such a precedent primordial state. However, that should not deter us from undertaking such a theoretical examination.

The Trinity Powers of Consciousness

One of the disappointing omissions within the creation story of Genesis is the absence of any commentary on our parent/creator. We are like adopted children, knowing that we have biological parents, yet knowing nothing about them; we don't know what they were like, whether they truly loved us, and, if so, why they abandoned us. So, let us contemplate what our parent/creator might be like—what attributes he may possess, and whether we, as his children, may have similar qualities encoded in our own DNA.

We can start with the preliminary assumption that all creation occurs through a combination of diverse elements. For example, the right combination of hydrogen and oxygen atoms leads to the creation of water. As basic as that model is, I believe that it provides an appropriate template for the discussion to follow. So let's consider what may be the diverse elements that, when bonded together, give us that all-encompassing and ineffable power that man identifies as his Creator, God.

Man attributes certain phenomenal characteristics as belonging exclusively to God. For instance, man believes that God is omnipresent, meaning that God is a presence everywhere at all times. Therefore, one of the extraordinary qualities to be found in our Creator is that which is infinite. Man also believes that God is omniscient, meaning that God is all knowing at all times. So, another attribute to be found in our Creator is that of an all-encompassing consciousness. Thus far, we have identified two attributes of the ineffable power we call God, which together we can identify as infinite consciousness. Man also believes that God is omnipotent, meaning that God is all-powerful at all times.

How may we view such an all-encompassing power? There are many definitions of power, most of which have to do with the exercise of control over persons or events. Such definitions are limiting and overly associated with human behavior. There is however, a power occasionally witnessed in human action that is so commanding of attention and is so powerful in expression that it electrifies the human spirit. It is a transcendent power, existing apart from and not subject to the limitations of selfish human behavior. That transcendent and all-encompassing power is called love. Not the love we equate with physical attraction or possession, but that selfless love that puts service to another before all other human considerations.

Such acts of selfless love are sometimes witnessed on the battlefield of war when, without a moment's hesitation, a man will sacrifice his own life in order to save the lives of his comrades. No greater love has ever been shown by man than that he lay down his very life for another. These selfless acts are called acts of 'uncommon valor' because such extraordinary and heroic acts are not a common occurrence in human behavior. Such acts of love are boundless and unconditional, and emanate not from physical man but from the spirit of man. Therefore, I will identify a boundless and unconditional love as the final power or expression to be found in that ineffable power we call God. Accordingly, we may come closer to knowing our parent/creator as that which he truly is, as infinite conscious love.

Before we go further in this discussion, we have to understand that what we are referring to as Infinite Conscious Love has no correlation to what we human beings experience as either consciousness or love. As human beings, we can never comprehend, let alone experience, that omniscient, omnipresent, and omnipotent primordial expression that is the infinite conscious love we call God, or more simply the conscious love of God. Man's understanding of such an ineffable power is severely limited by the restraints imposed upon his conscious awareness by the limitations of his five physical senses. Man presently lacks the intellectual and emotional maturity to fully comprehend, let alone experience, such transcendent realities.

The Trinity Powers of Consciousness, which collectively we identify as the infinite conscious love of God, coexist simultaneously and coequally, within an inseparable union. It is through the interactive union between Consciousness, representative of the Father, and Love, representative of the Mother that is born the son or Spirit of creation. This unity of expression is in fact the template upon which man, made in "the image and after the likeness of God," was created. It is Adam as the power of consciousness, Eve as the power of love, and the conscious union of the two that gives birth to their own son or spirit of creation. It is the spirit of creation born of the conscious union between Adam and Eve that allows for the fulfillment of God's directive to Adam and Eve to be fruitful and to multiply. It is a directive for the "two" to exercise their creative authority by becoming "one," through the harmonious union or marriage of their consciousness, infinitely and faithfully expressed. It was by such a creative union that Adam and Eve were to exercise dominion within the Garden of Eden, to dress and to keep it.

When infinite consciousness as the manifestation of the divine Masculine, and infinite love as the manifestation of the divine Feminine are united as one, they form the boundless reality that is the conscious love of God. Consciousness and Love as primordial powers have always existed without having been created, and each will never cease to exist. Together, Consciousness and Love form a flawless, perfect, and harmonious union. There is only the silent eternal embrace of all that ever was, is, or will be—that omnipresent, omniscient, and omnipotent everlasting eternal power and presence of the conscious love of God. All the many multi-layered realities of consciousness emerge and coexist by and through this flawless, perfect, and harmonious union of Consciousness and Love. The Trinity Powers of Consciousness, collectively the infinite conscious love of God, are the first cause for all that has ever been, is now, or ever will be. To be embraced within the bosom of the conscious love of God is to experience a state of profound bliss.

Man is unable to comprehend the magnitude of such an infinite conscious love. Although we have all experienced love, and have on occasion been witness to truly heroic acts of love, such experiences are but a very faint echo of the conscious love of God. We could never endure the intensity of the all-embracing conscious love of God. In such a state, we would be unable to hold on to our individual identity. Our sense of self would dissolve, and we would once again become one with the conscious love of God. We would simply exist in a perpetual state of bliss and ecstasy. This state of infinite conscious love is the one and only constant, unchangeable, indissoluble reality of which there is nothing greater and of which nothing lesser could ever challenge. It is a state of perfect and immutable balance and harmony. It is the source and wellspring of all creation.

For mortal minds, it is difficult to comprehend that infinite, deep, silent stillness, that state of nothingness and non-being that comprises all that ever was, is now, or ever will be. Much has been written on the central question of the origin of man and how the world began. It is a question still in search of an answer—an answer that requires looking through many veils, a capacity that man presently lacks. Even so, such limitations should not restrain our enthusiasm to undertake such a journey as we will, along the way, make some profound discoveries. So, let us take our inquiry further and explore the nature of the event that resulted in an explosion of movement and sound that gave birth to man and the universe.

The Union of Consciousness and Love

To aid our further discussion of that ineffable power we call the conscious love of God, it will be helpful to employ the Chinese philosophical concept of yin and yang. The concept behind yin and yang is that of two complementary yet opposing principles engaged in an interactive dance, the performance of which creates balance and harmony within the universe. Yin is viewed as the feminine principle, while yang is seen as the masculine principle. As in the analogy of yin and yang, consciousness and love are likewise engaged in a harmonious dance. Like two lovers in a courtship, consciousness as the masculine principle and love as the feminine principle eventually move on to a more permanent union. The union of these two principles results in a creative act that would not be possible in the absence of such a union.

At the moment of the bonding of their union, the precise manner of which we can only imagine, the silence of the eternal and blissful dance between consciousness and love was broken, and, in one critically intense nanosecond of time, consciousness and love became aware of their indivisible union; of the two being one. It was as if the light of consciousness—yang—had pierced the dark solitude of love—yin—resulting in an ecstatic shout that rippled throughout the infinite primordial ocean, shattering the silent stillness of the eternal void. Out of that climatic union was born the impulse of consciousness, as the active masculine principle of desire, and of love, as the passive feminine principle of feeling, to perpetually seek out one another to experience the bliss and ecstasy of their eternal union. Out of this bonded union between consciousness and love is born the spirit of Creation.

The result of this union between consciousness and love was not only the activation of a creative impulse, it was the initiation of the Mother/Father Principle and template for all of creation thereafter emerging within the primordial ocean we call the conscious love of God. It is this perfect union between love as the Mother Principle, and consciousness as the Father Principle, out of which all creation has, is, or ever will emanate. There is no creation emanating from the conscious love of God that is less than perfect. The conscious love of God is unaffected by that which may emanate from it. It always was, and will always be, even if our infinite universe is ignited in conflagration and disappears.

It is at this juncture that we need to be cautious in our effort not to personalize God. We must keep in mind that God, as infinite conscious love, cannot be defined. God is a presence and a power, not a personality. Whereas all things emanate from God, there can be nothing greater than God—not even the collectivity or perfection of all of his creations. All exists within the love-infused consciousness that is God. The underlying principle unifying all creation is the power of consciousness, infinitely infused with the power of love.

Admittedly, any discussion of such a primordial reality—about who is God and who is man—will always remain open. As a mortal being under the control of nature, man lacks the capacity to answer questions pertaining to the eternal with any degree of certainty. The lesser can never fully comprehend the greater. However, I believe that man, as the divine being that he truly is, and through the use of his higher senses of consciousness, can break the restraints imposed upon his thinking by his physical senses. I believe that man can reach beyond his limited temporal experience and dive into the waters of the primordial ocean of pure consciousness to once again experience that all-embracing presence and power we call God.

Man as the Atom of God Consciousness

Science speculates that all life emerged out of the sea. Whether resident within our physical reality or in realities yet inaccessible to man, all life does come from out of the sea, the sea of the conscious love we call God. Consciousness and love, as precedent primordial energy, has no beginning origin. It was itself not created; it has always existed and it will never cease to exist. There is nothing that can be added to that which is an all-knowing consciousness eternally bonded to an all-powerful love. The union of consciousness and love creates a state of bliss. In such a union consciousness and love are unaware of that which may emerge out of their eternal and blissful embrace. As primordial powers, consciousness and love are simply not moved by such considerations. However, it is only through the harmonious and balanced interactive union between these two ineffable powers—of consciousness infused with love, and love infused with consciousness—that creation is possible.

It is conscious love that links all creation to the same source, to the same Creator, to God. There is nothing emanating out of the primordial ocean of the conscious love of God that is not itself infused with conscious love. Each man created in the image and likeness of God as the Atom of God Consciousness is equal in potential, as each emanates out of the conscious love of God. However, not all such expressions of the conscious love of God, not all Atoms of God Consciousness are equal in the realization of their heritage as a child of God. Such realization is acquired only when the Atom of God

Consciousness evolves into a state of self-awareness and clothes itself with a physical body of light with an immortal soul. It is at that stage of evolution that man earns the privileged to then take on the mantle as a co-creator with God. The evolutionary journey of each Atom of God Consciousness can take an eternity to complete. That is because as a co-creator each Atom of God Consciousness is presented with an infinitely unlimited choice of options to experience the breadth and fullness of the conscious love of God. At the end of its journey, each Atom of God Consciousness will have mastered all that can be experienced as conscious love. It will then desire to return home to the sea that is the conscious love of God, there to enjoy the eternal bliss that can only be found within the loving embrace of God.

Each Atom of God Consciousness begins its journey as an individual expression of the conscious love of God, as an archetypal spirit form clothed in the illuminating light substance of consciousness. At the appropriate stage of its evolutionary development, each Atom of God Consciousness will take on the clothing of physical matter. This is the evolutionary path taken by all forms of creation emerging through the movement of the 'out-breath' of God. While on its journey of evolution, each Atom of God Consciousness remains simultaneously existent on all levels and densities of consciousness through which and into which it is made manifest. Therefore, and notwithstanding man's corruption of his divine consciousness and his fall into this envelope of time, space, and matter, he remains existent outside of that envelope of reality. All expressions of the conscious love of God simultaneously experience their existence throughout many spirit/matter realities of consciousness.

The ultimate redemption of man will occur when, recognizing that he is an Atom of God Consciousness, he once again gains mastery over his consciousness and exercises the proper use of the energy sustaining all life; the energy of the consciousness of love. Bringing about the successful marriage between consciousness and love will result in man's restoration of his incorruptible and immortal physical body of light, a body capable of the unimpeded movement between the various realms of spirit and matter within the Paradise called Eden. This transformation is already evident. As we view the physical evolution of man from a brutish ape-like creature to, by comparison, bordering on the angelic, we may assume the obvious outcome of man's intrusion into this temporal world will eventually be the restoration of his physical body into the incorruptible body of light—his immortal soul.

Where else in the realm of nature do we witness such a transformative change in the physical appearance of a species as that which has occurred in man? In comparison, the broad spectrum of animal life found within nature, in appearance and overall development, has remained relatively constant. None can dispute that the man of today is far removed in appearance from his ancestors, Neanderthal and Cro-Magnon Man, and those other presumed members of the hominids family, such as the ape, which preceded him. (I say "presumed" as I have often pondered whether the ape is not in fact the product of man's original sin and his failed sojourn in the realm of nature. Such an occurrence would still make the ape a relative, however, not in the way theorized by science.)

Hopefully, at this point in our dialogue, the reader will be ready to embrace the proposition that Garden of Eden was not located on our small planet of Earth. Eden will always exist outside of our three-dimensional reality of consciousness as a timeless world of permanence and perfection and true home to immortal man. Eden is a paradise comprising many spirit/matter realities of consciousness, of the many mansions existing throughout the Father's house (John 14:2) Our journey through this temporal world reality is all about the restoration of our imperishable body of light, our immortal soul. It is also about the restoration of our higher divine consciousness and our rightful role as co-creator with God. When ready, each soul will willingly undertake this journey of redemption. It is a journey that may take an eternity to complete, as it will be necessary for each soul to first master living in this three-dimensional reality of time, space, and matter. For man, like the 'prodigal son,' it is ultimately a journey home to reclaim our birthright as fully realized sons and daughters of God.

The Imperishable Body of Light That Is the Immortal Soul

Since antiquity poets, philosophers, and theologians have written extensively, although without any universal consensus, on the fundamental nature of what we call the immortal soul. Essentially, the soul has been defined as the spiritual character of man regarded as immortal and unaffected by death. However, I would define the soul as being the incorruptible and immortal body of light with which each Atom of God Consciousness was clothed when God placed his breath into the nostrils of the physical body of Adam. It is the Atom of God Consciousness, that image and likeness of God, that makes up the spiritual character of man. It is the incorruptible body of light called the soul that forever houses each Atom of God Consciousness. It is the Atom of God Consciousness clothed with an incorruptible body of light called the soul that distinguished the man Adam from every other expression of life within the Garden of Eden.

It is soul energy that forms the body matrix or template around which is drawn and magnetized the physical material substance to form the outer clothing to be worn by the numerous spirit forms of creation. Soul energy manifests as light matter and is the further coalescing and densification of the illuminating light of consciousness. The evolutionary process of spirit becoming one with matter could not occur without spirit first being clothed with the material light substance of soul energy.

All of the numerous expressions of life within the Garden of

Eden are formed of body, soul, and spirit. However, within man, the unity of body, soul, and spirit is unlike that of any other expression of life within Eden. It is only the spirit of man as the Atom of God Consciousness that bears the image and likeness of God. Each Atom of God Consciousness is clothed with a soul body composed of the substance of light matter and around which is drawn a material physical body composed of the dust of the ground. What distinguishes the soul of man from all others in creation is that the soul that clothes man's spirit was individualized when God placed his breath—the breath that is the energy that forms the soul body template—into the nostrils of man. By so individualizing the soul body template within man, God made man's soul, as well as the physical matter, which was magnetized around it, man's physical body of dust, immortal for all eternity.

All of the other expressions of life within nature are likewise composed of body, soul, and spirit. However, the spirit consciousness and soul templates for all of the other expressions of life within nature were not individualized as they were in man. All of the other spirit expressions of life within nature remain unified as a group consciousness resident within a group soul for the particular species within which such consciousness and soul energy manifest. All cattle, all horses, all fish and fowl respectively share the same unified consciousness and unified soul body template of their particular species. When members of a particular species die the material substance and the soul energy of their physical bodies are returned to nature. The elemental forces of nature then use the reclaimed energy and matter to weave new physical bodies to clothe the new expressions of spirit consciousness emerging out of the group consciousness of the particular species. This is how, through cycles of death and decay, the elemental forces of nature ensure the perpetuation of all of the various expressions of spirit consciousness within the realm of nature.

Unlike the numerous species within nature, man was never intended to recycle through nature. He was to exercise dominion over nature—to dress and keep it. When sustained by the fruit from the Tree of Life, the material physical body magnetized to the immortal soul body of the Atom of God Consciousness becomes an imperishable body, a self-regenerating body, an immortal body that will never die. Allegorically, the Tree of Life within Eden represents the balanced and harmonious conscious love of God. Adam and Eve were free to consume the nectar of the fruit of the Tree of Life, that is, the two were free to bind together as one their masculine and feminine polarities of consciousness. It is only in the binding together of the feminine and masculine polarities of consciousness that the material physical body of each divine couple can remain imperishable.

Man suffered a corruption of his divine consciousness after he had consumed nectar of the fruit of the Tree of Knowledge. The fruit of the Tree of Knowledge was like an intoxicant the effect of which was to dim man's conscious awareness. This dimming of consciousness led to a weakening and ultimately to a severance in the bonded union of consciousness between those divine couples who fell to the temptation to consume the forbidden fruit. The severance of their polarities of consciousness resulted in the corruption of their immortal soul body. With the loss of their divine consciousness and the corruption of their immortal soul body, these fallen Adams and Eves each became trapped in a material physical body and bound to the laws and cycles of nature.

Allegorically, the Tree of Knowledge within Eden represents the elemental consciousness of change and transition; that is the cycling of the light matter of creation into the infinite diversity of life to be found within nature. By consuming the fruit of the Tree of Knowledge, man not only corrupted his body of light, his immortal soul. He also allowed his physical body to fall under the control and dominion of the elemental forces within nature, to the cycling of matter within nature. In order for each of us to return to the immortal life experience we once enjoyed in the Paradise of Eden we must redeem our immortal soul by restoring the unity of consciousness between the masculine and feminine that is the foundation of each Atom of God Consciousness, each Adam and Eve.

We Are All Sons and Daughters of God

God our Creator is not a supreme being sitting on a heavenly perch orchestrating the events in man's life. God, as an ever-eternal, unchanging presence and the foundation upon which stands all reality is so much more. Man's efforts to personalize God only serve to limit the wondrous reality that is God. That power and presence we identify as God cannot be contained within the words of man, and certainly cannot be co-opted by any one religious denomination to the exclusion of all others. Nevertheless, as a child may embrace its parent, God remains ever-embraceable by man.

How may we view the formation of this parent/child relationship between God and man? Regrettably, Genesis offers us no insight into that profound question. At best, we can only theorize an answer. The theory I wish to advance is that, at the profound moment when infinite Consciousness and infinite Love awoke to their indivisible union, there arose a mutual desire to experience one another in an eternal embrace. And from out of their indissoluble and blissful union was born the desire to perpetually give birth to the Spirit of Creation as the limitless expression of its unified self. And like waves rolling across an endless ocean, the Spirit of Creation is perpetually and endlessly being born out of the eternal embrace between Consciousness and Love. And as a wave can never fully comprehend the magnitude of the ocean of which it is a part, so too is it with each expression born of the union between Consciousness and Love, modeled in its image and likeness as the Atom of God

Consciousness—as man.

As individuated expressions of the infinite conscious love of God, the relevant question becomes: how should we perceive our relationship with God? Unfortunately, the religions of the world tend to personalize God with human characteristics. So God becomes more like a stern father constantly reprimanding his unruly children. God is seen as a judge inflicting all sorts of punishments for misbehavior and evaluating each of his children as to their entitlement to the reward of heaven or the punishment of hell. Personalizing God in such a way has severely handicapped man's ability to establish a truly meaningful relationship with his Creator.

Unlike man, God is not a person, nor a personality. To experience the ineffable power and presence we identify as God is to know that there is nothing greater than to experience the infinite conscious love of God. There are no beginnings or endings when embraced within the infinite conscious love of God. There certainly are no judgments or punishments. The state or condition of the love we call God is flawless, being incapable of anger or judgment. All things emanating from the infinite conscious love of God—and in particular man, as the offspring of God—are perfect. God, in a constant and immutable state of conscious love, simply and endlessly expresses a perfect and limitless love. Are we really to believe that God, as the expression of such perfect love, would establish a program whereby good men would go to heaven and bad men would go to hell? Of course not—that is how man thinks, not God. Yet man has the capacity to think as God thinks. After all, is not man created in the image and after the likeness of God, as an Atom of God Consciousness?

But consciousness alone does not distinguish nor make man unique within creation. To the extent that a single-celled amoeba reacts to external stimuli, it arguably has an awareness or consciousness of something. The quality of consciousness that distinguishes man from all else within creation and that allows man to move beyond a simple awareness into self-awareness is his ability to exercise choice. It is only by the right exercise of choice in the use of the energy of the consciousness of love that man can evolve his conscious awareness and thereby move closer to a greater comprehension of and union with the infinite conscious love of God. Man's relationship to God is likened to that of a drop of water out of an ocean, or that of a child to a parent. Each is born of the greater, but lacks the capacity of the greater. For man, it is all about the evolutionary journey back to the fullness and perfection that is the love of God. It is a journey aided or hindered by choice.

In My Father's House

Jesus said, "In my Father's house are many mansions" (John 14.2). I believe that what Jesus was referring to were the many levels of creation flowing out of the union between Consciousness and Love, infinitely expressed as the Spirit of Creation. Consciousness is the foundation upon which the many transcendent and cosmic realities stand. It is through the never-ending evolution of consciousness that 'intelligent design' emerges within the many levels of creation. Each of the levels of creation comprises but one of an infinite number of cascading waves or realities, and each are but one unique expression of that perfect reality we call the infinite conscious love of God. There truly are many levels or "mansions" emanating as an expression of the consciousness love of God.

These many levels of creation are like unmarked tablets of clay upon which the out-breath of God has engraved itself. Each expression of the conscious love of God is on its own journey of evolution, of expanding its inherent consciousness to levels of greater complexity. The journey for man as an Atom of God Consciousness is to evolve his consciousness into a self-conscious awareness. He achieves this evolution through the right use of the energy of the consciousness of love. The right use of the energy of the consciousness of love leads to the acquisition of wisdom. It is only with the acquisition of wisdom that each Son and Daughter of God can come to truly know and experience the full breadth of God.

However, initially each nascent Atom of God Consciousness

lacks the capacity for self-directed activity. As a nascent Atom of God Consciousness, man is likened to the angels, who are simply representative beings of God's infinite love and who can only act out of perfect love. Like the angels, each nascent Atom of God Consciousness cannot choose to do otherwise. It is not until a nascent Atom of God Consciousness has acquired the capacity to choose that it can evolve into a consciousness that is self-aware. It is only through the right use of the energy of the consciousness of love that an Atom of God Consciousness can evolve into greater levels of conscious self-awareness and thereby earn the privilege of becoming a co-creator with God.

As each Atom of God journeys through successive levels or degrees of consciousness, he acquires a wealth of experience that leads to wisdom. When each fully realized Atom of God Consciousness again merges with the infinite conscious love of God, the wisdom acquired in the right use of the consciousness of love will become part of the infinite love of God. Creation is a perpetually self-sustaining cycle with each 'out-breath of God' creating individuated and limitless expressions of itself. Within each 'in-breath of God' is contained the profundity of experience and wisdom acquired through the expansion of conscious awareness of each of the individuated expressions of God. The breath of God is eternal; it will never end.

All of the infinite levels of creation are interrelated with one another—each flowing out of the same source—the infinite conscious love of God. Each expression of the conscious love of God riding the in-breath back to God now has a greater level of conscious awareness of its individuation as an essence of God and thus a greater comprehension of God. And like riding a comet's tail, those expressions of God further away from reunion with God are carried along and supported by those individuated expressions of conscious love that preceded them. All expressions of the infinite conscious love of God are acting independently of one another, yet collectively acting as co-creators with God in never-ending cycles of creation.

The fact that the universe is composed of the energy of the conscious love of God remains an enigma to both science and religion. The material world is simply the energy of the conscious love of God coalesced into form and dressed in matter. The movement or vibration of the energy that is the Consciousness of God is the sole cause for the manifestation, formation, and densification of all matter. The energy that is the Consciousness of God, moving at its highest vibration, is pure light. The unqualified energy that is God is pure light. The Consciousness of God, being the highest possible vibration, comprises a light so bright that physical man could never stand in its presence and retain his present physical form. Any such material, physical body would simply be consumed within the intensity of such light. As the movement of the energy of God slows and as the voice of God softens into lower vibrational ranges, the energy of God coalesces around a diversity of archetypal spirit forms. And through the further coalescence of the energy of God, the diversity of archetypal spirit forms take on the clothing of physical matter. The physical universe is the outcome of the soft voice of God echoing out of the climactic and sacred union between infinite Love as Mother and infinite Consciousness as Father, being cast outward in ever-expanding waves of never-ending creation.

Comprehension of the mystery of creation is beyond man's present level of consciousness. Man sees and understands events in linear fashion, and then only as framed by his physical senses, then only as translated within the limiting environment of nature. That process has worked well enough within our particular envelope of time, space, and matter. However, we should not assume within realities of consciousness less dense than our own that we would experience time, space, and matter as we now do. That yardstick may be totally inapplicable, particularly in a reality where time, space, and matter may offer a unified experience and not one of separation as in our own. Ultimately, we may discover that, instead of space, there may simply be the energy of consciousness, instead of time there may only be the eternal moment, and instead of physical matter there may only be light.

Man needs to understand that what he can explain only by the measure of time within an envelope of space occurs instantaneously in the reality that is the infinite conscious love of God. The unfolding of the universe commenced at that same timeless moment that the conscious love of God expressed as light emerged out of that sacred union between infinite Love and infinite Consciousness. This timeless and eternal unfolding of creation continued throughout infinite and successive waves of ever-expanding circles of light energy to that point where the vibrational energy, the sounds arising out of the intimate union between Consciousness and Love, gave birth to our infinite universe.

Creation occurred outside of time and space as currently understood, by us. Therefore, outside of our experience of time our infinite universe would have unfolded, not in the 13 billion or more years theorized by science, but instantaneously. Science is simply measuring the vibrational rate of the light of creation as it travels within our virtual holographic three-dimensional envelope of time and space. Time is irrelevant in creation. All that was, is, or ever will be occurred in that moment when infinite Love and infinite Consciousness awoke to their indivisible and blissful union. Both the Big Bang theory of science and the theory put forth by the creationists are valid propositions to explain the formation of the perceptible world. It is now time for man to merge those two separate theories into one comprehensive model of creation.

The light of the conscious love of God that manifests at the farthest reaches from the center of creation is no less perfect or complete and remains as capable of continued evolution as the light manifesting at the center. It is still the ecstatic shout of the Mother and Father of Creation, giving the energy of their breath of life to the Spirit of Creation. It is an ecstatic shout heard throughout all the many mansions of our Father's house.

As the vibration of the sound of the ecstatic shout of the Mother and Father of Creation expands outward, it softens; first giving birth to the spirit realms of the Heaven and the Earth, and then evolving into the matter realm of the Paradise of Eden. It is in the Paradise of Eden that each divine couple, each Adam and Eve, as the self-conscious expression of the love of God, exercises their role as co-creators. In compliance with the directive to be fruitful and multiply they engage in the creation of the myriad forms and expressions of life to be found throughout the many "mansions" or levels of consciousness within the Paradise of Eden. "And God blessed them, and God said unto them, Be fruitful, and multiply, and replenish the earth, and subdue it..." (Genesis 1:28).

The farther we get from the center of creation, the softer becomes the sound or vibration of creation. The softer the sound or vibration of creation, the greater is the potential for the energy of God to be molded into infinite forms and infinite realities. All the individuated expressions of God are constantly striving to become one in conscious love with the conscious love of God. As a drop of the ocean can never fully comprehend the ocean of which it is a part, so too it is with each individual Atom of God Consciousness emerging out of the greater Consciousness of God. However, through the collective and shared experiences gained in the evolution of consciousness, each Atom of God Consciousness can gain a greater understanding of the reality that is the conscious love of God.

We must never lose sight of the fact that all is God, and all that we can experience has emanated from God. Any suggestion that man, as the softest expression of the sound of God, is thereby less than the loudest expression would be to imply the existence of limitation in the reality that is God. God simply cannot be greater and lesser at the same time. Likewise, God cannot be more perfect and less perfect at the same time. God can only be perfect at all times in all of his manifestations. However, it is the task of all such manifestations, including man, to awaken to the sound and movement of the Spoken Word of God, as together we all ride on the in-breath of God.

Prelude to the Fall of Man's Divine Consciousness

A ll creation emanates out of the interactive union between light and darkness, of Consciousness and Love. Out of this union is born the Spirit of Creation as the illuminating light of consciousness. Throughout all the many mansions of our Father's house time, space, and matter form a cohesive unity. Within that unity there is only the experience of the unfolding of the illuminating light of consciousness—of the Spirit of Creation, as it moves within the infinite sea of the Consciousness of God. It is through the movement of this illuminating light of consciousness, as the Spirit of Creation, that the greater complexities of creation manifest. In that regard, the creationists do stand on solid ground. However, when we enter the temporal realm, that envelope of time, space, and matter we call our infinite universe, creationists must share the ground of the evolution of spirit within matter with the scientists. Likewise, scientists must recognize that what is here called the temporal realm flows from out of the timeless realm of spirit, that infinite yet ever-expanding reality we call the conscious love of God.

Within the confines of the universe, man sees himself as unique, believing that he is the only consciously self-aware and self-directed being. I personally do not believe that we are alone in the universe, but for those who do, the obvious question is: to what end did God create this infinite universe? Most scientists believe that we will never develop the means to leave our own solar system, let alone traverse our own galaxy. As we know, there are billions of galaxies out there, and possibly unlimited universes as well.

Such considerations raise the question of whether it was ever intended that there be a temporal reality—a world of time, space, and matter such as that which we now occupy. Genesis suggests that the answer may be yes, as we are told that God exiled Adam and Eve to such a world. However, prior to the exile, there was no mention in Genesis of such a temporal and changing world reality. Likewise, we know from Genesis that while he resided in the Garden of Eden, man's physical body did not suffer death. Not until he was exiled from Eden did man's body, now clothed in "coats of skins" become subject to decay and death. "For dust thou [art,] and unto dust shalt thou return" (Genesis 3:19).

I have contended that Adam, the man of Eden, was created and formed as a threefold being consisting of a spirit consciousness clothed with a soul, a material body of light around which was magnetized an imperishable physical body. Since man's expulsion from Eden his physical body is no longer imperishable, but now goes through a period of decline that eventually leads to death. But upon the death of the body, what are we to presume then happens to the soul and spirit of man? Is the physical death of the body a final ending? Or is death simply a period of intermission taken by the soul and spirit between acts in the much larger play of the redemptive journey?

When you take a physical cube of sugar and drop it into a glass of water it loses its physical form. We can say that the cube, the body of sugar, has died. Nevertheless, the essence of sugar, its sweetness, still exists in its now altered and unseen state. It has simply moved into another reality, subject to reappearing as a cube of sugar when the proper process of sugar creation is employed. Likewise, when a man dies and his physical body is placed in the ground, it too dissolves. Nevertheless, does not the soul and spirit, the essence and consciousness of man, still exist? Something must exist, otherwise there would be no relevancy to any discussion of heaven or hell.

And how are we to view the paradise Garden of Eden? Is it reasonable to believe that the earth of Genesis refers to our home planet and that the paradise Garden of Eden was located somewhere in the Mediterranean? In searching for answers to such questions, it again becomes necessary to view Genesis as an allegorical account of creation. The Earth and Eden of Genesis are representative of the twin states of spirit and matter each emerging out of the infinite conscious love of God. Together, Eden and Earth form an inseparably unified and transcendent reality.

However, our universe, unlike the timeless and permanent reality that is the paradise of Eden, is a realm in which we perceive a separation between space and time, and in which we witness the constant disintegration of physical matter. Prior to Eden, there was only the heaven and the earth as a realm of spirit. Through a coalescence and densification of the substance of light matter, the spirit form of the Earth was clothed with physical matter, becoming the paradise of Eden. Eden then became the forum for the further evolution of the Atom of God Consciousness, now represented in the man, Adam, and the woman, Eve.

The world outside of Eden and into which man was exiled was created not by God, but by man. Man created this temporal world through the corruption of his higher divine consciousness, which lead to the corruption of the perfect order, of the perfect balance and harmony within Eden. This temporal world of decay continues to be held together solely by the continuing corruption of man's higher consciousness. The consequence of man's fall has been the creation of a three-dimensional reality in which life is played out within a virtual or holographic environment. The reality that we all experience is that of a dream. The only doorway back into Eden is through the restoration of the balance and harmony of man's higher divine consciousness.

So how did man get from the idyllic paradise of Eden and enjoyment of physical immortality to the temporal world we now occupy with a physical body that decays and dies? As a resident of Eden, man was endowed with dominion over the realm of nature, "over all living things that moveth upon the earth" (Genesis 1:28). However, in furtherance of man's evolution as a co-creator with God, it was necessary for man to come to know and understand all that was within nature within the Garden of Eden. Only by understanding nature could man wisely exercise dominion over it. Regrettably, for many of us, this journey into nature was a failure, resulting in man's so-called fall from grace and the loss of the light of his God consciousness. Man truly fell into darkness. This fall into darkness was the outcome of choices freely made.

The ineffable power we call God is infinite conscious love. Although the source of all that was, is, or ever will be, God is not moved in any fashion or by any force to exercise dominion or control over any element of creation. God is content to simply be that perpetual state of blissful solitude. It is within the undulating movement of the endless waves flowing from out of the Consciousness of God that we witness the diversity of the evolution of consciousness within creation. It will be through many lifecycles and the experiences gained that each of us will eventually succeed in the restoration of our higher consciousness. With the restoration of our divine consciousness we will once again enjoy the eternal experience found only in the unity of time, space, and matter. It is a unity of experience that can only be found in the right use of the energy of the consciousness of love.

To experience the presence of God is to experience the all-encompassing power of infinite conscious love. Like fish in an ocean, all expressions of life swim in an endless sea of creative potential. As we pull anchor and leave the shore of the temporal world to sale upon the sea of creative potential, we notice that the material world dissolves into more delicate forms of light and energy. As we continue on our journey these forms of light and energy give way to spirit forms all emerging from within the deep infinite sea that is the conscious love of God. And so it is that within the Consciousness of God the blueprint for all that was, is, or ever will be, originates. The outcome of the unfolding of the blueprint of creation within the Consciousness of God leads to the creation of the realm of permanence called the paradise of Eden.

Within the paradise of Eden to think is to create, to be fruitful, and to multiply. However, in his fallen state of conscious awareness, man lacks the capacity to create through an act of consciousness. Man's level of conscious awareness is no longer sufficiently powerful to exercise control over the forces of nature. Our capacity to engage in conscious thought has become impeded as a consequence of the perceived separation between time, space, and matter, and by the limitations inherent in only using our five physical senses. We have lost not only the knowledge of the unity between time, space, and matter; we have also lost all awareness of our many higher nonphysical senses.

This dimming of our conscious awareness has transformed our reality into one of duality, of opposites, and of negativity. As in the paradise of Eden, creation of life within our temporal realm is likewise achieved through the coming together of pairs and opposites. However, unlike within Eden, man's ability to create is not initiated through any exercise of dominion or control over the forces of nature, and least of all through any act of consciousness. More accurately, creation by man within nature now occurs primarily through his insatiable consumption of the sensual energy that pervades the very atmosphere within nature. As a consequence, it is now the forces of nature that exercise dominion and control over the consciousness of man and over man's physical body.

The Tree of Life from which man could eat freely is representative of the source and wellspring of the energy of the consciousness of love. It is in the consumption or the right use of the energy of the consciousness of love that man, as the Atom of God Consciousness wearing the garment of an immortal body called a soul, is insured the perpetual residency in the Paradise called Eden. In that perfected state of the consciousness of love, man enjoyed unlimited happiness and the unrestricted ability to create, to be fruitful and multiply. Nevertheless, it is the journey of every immortal soul to expand its conscious self-awareness.

All expressions of God seek not only to create but also to experience that which has been created. In so doing, wisdom is acquired. It is an undertaking that occupies every Atom of God Consciousness as it seeks to discover and to come to know the wholeness of the love that is God. However, this can only be accomplished through the exercise of choice in the right use of the energy of the consciousness of love—such independence in the exercise of choice cannot be acquired by man as an androgynous being with a unified masculine/feminine polarity of consciousness. In such a state, man is like the angels who, lacking the freedom of choice, simply act out of the selfless and perfect conscious love of God.

For the further evolution of the Atom of God Consciousness, such freedom of choice could only be acquired by the bifurcation of the masculine and feminine polarities of consciousness resident within the androgynous Adam. Once the masculine and feminine polarities of consciousness had been separated into two independent physical bodies, each would then enter into nature now as a male and a female. It is within the realm of nature that the Atom of God Consciousness, now as the male Adam and the female Eve, can come to understand the laws of nature, particularly as they relate to the sexes within nature. To gain such understanding and thereby exercise dominion over nature requires the proper understanding of the Tree of Knowledge and the fruit it provides.

However, it was never intended that, in their undertaking to gain knowledge of the laws of nature, Adam and Eve would choose to consume the fruit of the Tree of Knowledge. Eating of this so-called fruit represents consumption of the sensual energy within nature. It is through the consumption of the sensual energy within nature that the lower orders of the beasts of the field are not only physically sustained, but that survival of the many species within nature is assured. The inevitable effect upon Adam and Eve in consuming the sensual fruit of nature was that, over time, they suffered a loss or dimming of the light of their higher divine consciousness. With their fall in consciousness Adam and Eve were no longer capable of sustaining their imperishable physical bodies. The fallen eventually became lost within the sea of sensual energy that is nature.

The greater number of divine couples, of Adam and Eves, were successful in their journey into nature and they continue to enjoy the fruit of the Tree of Life within the many realities of consciousness that comprise the paradise of Eden. For those of us divine couples who were not faithful to said undertaking, our life experience has been one of intense conflict between our higher divine consciousness and satisfying our insatiable physical sensual appetites. It is a battle between the light of our divine consciousness, and the darkness of what has become our mortal and selfish human nature. The marriage of our higher consciousness with the lower consciousness of the elementals within nature has been, to date, an unsuccessful marriage. The question we will explore is: how do we make this marriage work to create a path back to Eden?

PART IV

The Game of Life

A Parable

Together we have journeyed a long way in our discussion of the dynamics of creation, of man's origin, and of his relationship with God. And yet, there is still much ground to cover as we strive for even greater understanding of our celestial home of Eden and why we chose to leave it. There are many ways to examine man's temporal life experience within the broader context of his reality as an evolving Atom of God Consciousness. I would like to use the following parable as an introduction to the remainder of my discussion on man's journey back to Eden. It is my hope that this short allegorical story will help set the stage and aid readers as we continue to explore man's evolutionary journey as the Atom of God Consciousness.

~

As is customary at the end of every celestial day in the eternal realm of Eden, a group of young souls have gathered for some fun and relaxation at the local Heavenly Light Café. The conversation at the Café is all about a new and exciting interactive holographic game. Those who have looked into the game say that it is played by stepping into an artificially created, three-dimensional expanse. There are no naturally occurring three-dimensional states within the vast and diversified realities of Eden. That is because everything within the eternal realm of Eden is bound together in a cohesive and harmonious unity of time, space, and matter. This unity of time, space, and matter also allows for a shared consciousness among all who reside in Eden. Such a cohesive unity between time, space, matter, and consciousness is not feasible within the structural limitations of a three-dimensional state. Preliminary game reviews report that it is the difficulties posed by functioning within such a non-unified and virtual reality that make the game both challenging and exciting.

The goal of this game is to successfully engage in various acts of creation without violating Eden's universal law of creation. That law requires that all creation undertaken within the many realities of Eden occur only through the right and proper use of the 'energy' of creation. That energy is the energy that flows out of the 'conscious- ness of love.' If one can successfully play this game without incurring any penalties, one can accumulate much-desired wisdom. In Eden, wisdom is highly sought after, since only by the accumulation of wis- dom can a young soul hope to achieve the ultimate experience—a personal meeting with the master Creator of Eden, God. The poten- tial rewards earned in successfully playing the game are offset by the severe consequences for violating the rules of the game. Although just a game, the consequences can be so severe as to adversely affect a soul's evolutionary progress.

Some of the young souls at the Café are eager to play. Others want nothing to do with this new game, arguing that they already have a great life in Eden where everyone is of a youthful age, and immortal. Furthermore, Eden is a magnificent paradise where the weather is always pleasant, there are varied and delicious fruits to eat, and one can freely roam and explore Eden's many wonders. However, those young souls who are eager to take on the challenge remind their hesitant friends that the primary goal of every soul is to evolve their consciousness to higher levels and thereby acquire wisdom. Wisdom is the essential attribute necessary for a soul's evolution in conscious awareness, and for the right and proper use of the energy of creation. When acquired, wisdom allows a soul the privilege of participating with God in the endless cycles of creation throughout the eternal realm of Eden.

Within the realm of Eden the journey of a soul's evolution in conscious awareness proceeds at a very slow rate. That is because Eden is a perfectly unified reality that affords little opportunity for young souls to be challenged in the right and proper use of the en- ergy of creation. That has now changed with the invention by the

Wise Ones of the Game of Life, a holographic Genesis program in which participation can lead to the accumulation of wisdom at a highly-accelerated pace.

Through a manipulation of time, space, and matter, the Wise Ones have created a unique holographic environment that they have populated with many varied forms of plant and animal life. They call this game environment the realm of nature. In Eden time, space, and matter form an inseparable unity and everyone feels a very direct and personal connection to one another. However, within the Game of Life time, space, and matter are made to appear as separate and unrelated states. The apparent separation of the unity between time, space, and matter creates the illusion of the forward movement of time. This linear movement of time creates the further illusion that space, and the objects within space, exists outside of the flow of time. The result of these illusions leads the game participants to believe that they are both physically and consciously separated from one another as they move through the stream of time within the game environment. This seeming separation occurring between objects within space and moving through time is perceived to be real by the game participants. The game is a virtual reality, however, a grand illusion unfolding only within the consciousness of the game participant. And no two game participants will experience this grand illusion in the same way.

Although at any given time there are numerous participants in the game, the Game of Life is a single player game. Participants compete only against themselves as they move through time and space. The challenge faced by every game participant is to successfully replenish the varied plant and animal life within the game environment—in other words, to create. In order to succeed in that undertaking, the game participant must, through the proper use of the energy of consciousness, re-establish the unity between time, space, and matter. It is only by the successful manipulation of time, space, and matter while in the game environment that a game participant can evolve his conscious self-awareness, accumulate wisdom, and become a successful Creator.

There are, however, challenges facing each game participant upon entering the game. In addition to the numerous soul participants, who at any given time are also playing the game, the game is populated with a variety of nature beings called Elementals. The function of these elemental beings is to act as tailors, weaving together the threads of physical matter to be worn as clothing by the various plant and animal life forms found within the game environment. To become masters of the game, participants must develop the ability to control and direct the actions of these elemental beings. The Elementals lack any conscious self-awareness or the ability to self-initiate action. They are a neutral force within the game, programmed to willingly receive direction from the game participants. So long as game participants properly direct and control the activities of these elemental beings, they will not only succeed in mastering the game, but in so doing they will become full-fledged Creators. However, improperly directing or inappropriately interacting with these elemental beings can severely handicap a player's performance and lead to unpleasant if not unintended consequences.

Each game participant is allowed to enter the game with all of their divine endowments. The greatest challenge facing a game participant is that of choice. In order to be successful while in the game, all actions, all choices, have to be undertaken through the proper use of the energy of creation, the energy of the consciousness of love. Abiding by this one primary rule not only ensures winning the game, but also of accumulating much sought-after wisdom. However, if a game participant violates the primary rule of the game by improperly using the energy of creation for self-interest or to satisfy self-desire, a penalty is incurred. No game participant can exit the game until all penalties incurred have been removed.

There are many challenging exercises in the art of creation to undertake while in the game. However, the first challenge a game participant faces upon entering the game is the need to fashion a physical game body to wear over their more delicate body of light, their soul body. Such a physical body is necessary in order to stay in and play the game. Game participants undertake the creation of a game body by commanding and directing the elemental beings to weave an appropriate material body to clothe their natural body of light. However, prior to entering the game, each participant is cautioned not to engage in any personal interplay with the elemental beings. Game participants are told that the only interaction they should have with the elemental beings is to marshal and direct them in the creation process. In other words, they are instructed that so long as they remain in the game they should exercise full and complete dominion over these elemental beings. More importantly, game participants are told that if they were to engage in any interplay with the elemental beings during the creation of their game bodies, the elementals would become active within the participant's game body. This would result in the game participant experiencing sensations within their physical game body. Once sensations have been activated within a game participant's physical body, the elemental beings would continue to seek out such physical sensations.

In fact, it is the elemental beings seeking physical sensations that serve as the catalyst for the continued propagation and clothing of all of the expressions of life, of all living things that have been programmed into the game environment. Game participants are cautioned to always remember that they are not part of the game program. The game program is simply a tool designed to allow participants to try their hand at creation through the right and proper use of the energy of creation. Should a game participant fail to heed the caution not to experience sensations within their physical game body then sensations will become an addictive drug to their game body. And as with any addictive drug, the user will seek more and more of the sensational drug to satisfy their addictive need. Once a game participant has gone that far, he or she will have lost control not only over the creation process, but over their game body as well. The elemental beings will then have gained control over the game participant's physical body. They will then view the game participant's physical body as no different from the physical bodies that they have woven for all of the other lower categories of life within the game environment. That is why all game participants are cautioned not to fall to the temptation to experience sensations with their physical game body as to do so would be a violation of the right and proper use of the energy of creation.

Yielding to the temptation to experience sensations within one's physical game body would make it very difficult for a game participant to successfully complete the game. That is because once the Elementals have taken control of a game participant's physical body the participant's divine endowments, their extraordinary mental and psychic endowments would slowly begin to diminish. This would eventually lead to a substantial loss in the game participant's conscious self-awareness. The few sensors incorporated into the game participant's physical body would then be the only means by which the game participant could maneuver and function within the game environment. At that point the game participant would no longer be playing the game. He would have become part of the game. Once a game participant has fallen that far under the control of the elemental beings, it becomes difficult to kick the addiction to physical sensations. Of course, everyone who is thinking about taking on the challenge of the game proudly boasts that they can easily handle such tremendous challenges.

There are yet other dangers within the game for those who fall to the temptation to experience sensations in their game body. So long as the game participant maintains dominion over the elemental beings and does not inappropriately interact with them, his game body will remain imperishable for so as long as he chooses to remain in the game. However, once under the control of the elemental beings the game participant will begin to notice that his or her game body begins to deteriorate. That is a process built into the game and the manner by which the elemental beings continuously cycle and regenerate physical matter within the game environment. To the game participant, the body is of the utmost importance since, without a physical body, a participant would have to leave the game. While in the game some participants will devise many ingenious ways, in unsuccessful attempts, to prevent their game bodies from aging and disintegrating, but nothing they do can reverse this process. Furthermore, the time each participant is allotted to play any round of the game is limited and game participants are not told prior to entering the game just how much time they have been allotted to play a round of the game.

The limitations imposed upon the game participants were intended to present tremendous challenges. The Wise Ones knew that with numerous game participants so challenged, it was inevitable that some participants would fall, giving rise to conflict, negativity, and self-desire within the game environment, within nature. It is the choices made in such an environment, and in particular the choice to always act out of the consciousness of love and not the consciousness of sensation—of self-desire that is the challenge. Right choices are rewarded with an accumulation of wisdom. Bad choices result in a violation of the universal law of creation and will incur the accumulation of penalties. And an individual can accumulate many penalties in just one round of the game.

The Wise Ones, knowing the challenges of the game would be substantial, allowed for a limited degree of assistance from individuals outside of the game who wish to sponsor and support the game participants. These game assistants cannot themselves enter the game. They can only consciously direct guidance to the game participants. So long as each game participant maintains the unity of consciousness they were endowed with they can easily receive the assistance offered. However, it is contingent upon each player to consciously be receptive of such help. Unfortunately, many who have fallen under the control of the Elementals are not receptive because in their sensually addicted and dulled conscious states they are unaware of the help being offered.

If a participant is not happy with the penalties they have accumulated while playing the game they cannot simply walk away from the game. Therein lies the risk to all who choose to participate. A participant cannot be done with the game until all accumulated penalties have been removed. It is each fallen participant's obligation to reclaim their game body from the controlling forces of the elemental beings. Each such participant must also restore the balance and harmony of the universal law of creation that they disrupted while in the game.

At the end of every round of the game, the participants are allowed to temporarily exit and return to their normal state of conscious self-awareness for a period of extended rest before going back into the game. With the guidance of the Wise Ones, each participant's performance in the game is reviewed. There is no judgment, criticism, or condemnation as to the choices made in the game. Such negative attitudes are simply not sustainable in the in the celestial realm of Eden. All recognize that the game is merely a vehicle for the accelerated accumulation of wisdom. In fact, all who participate in the game are greatly admired for their tremendous courage in taking on such a high-risk challenge knowing that they may, through repeated bad choices, find themselves committed to the Game of Life for a very, very long time.

The Evolutionary Journey of the Atom of God Consciousness

Man, as an Atom of God Consciousness, is just one of the many emanations of conscious energy flowing from out of the infinite sea that is the conscious love of God. However, not all of these emanations are equal in degree or level of conscious awareness. It is only in a journey that begins by riding the wave of the out-breath of the Consciousness of God that the many emanations of consciousness can evolve into higher states of consciousness. And, as in the pull of a magnet, each of the many emanations of consciousness will eventually be drawn back to the deep waters that are the conscious love of God. It is in the journey of returning, of riding the in-breath of the Consciousness of God that the many emanations of consciousness, and in particular, man, as an Atom of God Consciousness, evolve into even higher states of conscious self-awareness.

Throughout the ages seers, mystics, and adepts have offered man guidance on how he may restore his fallen consciousness. Even so, such guidance is only effective to the degree that each of us is consciously receptive to it. Unfortunately, man, as a fallen consciousness, is unaware that he is an Atom, born from out of the infinite sea that is the Consciousness of God. As a consequence, man's restoration of his fallen consciousness has been painfully slow and incredibly arduous. To accelerate our journey back to Eden all we need to do is to awaken our higher consciousness.

To awaken our higher consciousness, we first need to understand that there is only one universal reality, and that reality is the infinite conscious love of God. Everything emanates from out of the sea that is the infinite conscious love of God. And everything that emerges out of that sea is clothed in the energy of the consciousness of love. There are, however, differing levels or degrees in the energy of consciousness. We can use the analogy of a burning flame to make the point. Just as the heat at the center of the flame is the most intense, burns the hottest, and consumes the fastest, the flame at the periphery also consumes that with which it comes in contact. It is merely a difference of degree of intensity. The intrinsic nature of the flame is uniform throughout.

The infinite conscious love of God is uniform throughout all of the multifaceted levels of creation. Even within our three-dimensional holographic environment the energy of consciousness is uniform throughout the four kingdoms of nature. Yet the degree of conscious awareness is greater in the plant kingdom than in the mineral, greater in the animal kingdom than the plant, and greater yet in the human kingdom than that of the animal. The energy that is the infinite conscious love of God is the potter's clay with which all that emanates from out of the Consciousness of God is fashioned. It is in the forming and shaping of this potter's clay that all the many and varied manifestations of the energy of consciousness evolve into even greater expression. And each evolving level of consciousness plays an indispensable role in the management of what is a multifaceted and truly infinite reality. The evolution of consciousness is a self-sustaining cycle of creation having no beginning and no end. The precision, balance, harmony, and perfection contained within the infinite conscious love of God are beyond mortal man's comprehension.

Man, as the evolving Atom of God Consciousness, was truly created in the "image and likeness" of God. In Act I of Genesis, God does not name man, only acknowledging that he "...created man in his [own] image, in the image of God created he him; male and female created he them" (Genesis 1:27). Man first emerged as an Atom of God, as an individuated unit of God consciousness. This Atom of God was a perfectly balanced androgynous being composed of a unified masculine and feminine polarity of consciousness, but lacking in conscious self-awareness. Initially, the androgynous man enjoyed the blissful and harmonious union of its bonded masculine and feminine polarities. However, the further evolution of the androgynous man required a separation between its masculine and the feminine polarities. It was only through the bifurcation of the Atom of God Consciousness that the masculine polarity of consciousness as the man, Adam, and the feminine polarity of consciousness as the woman, Eve, were each able to independently experience a conscious self-awareness. However, it was always intended that while in the bifurcated state of consciousness, Adam and Eve would nevertheless continue to act as one unified consciousness. For the further evolution of the Atom of God Consciousness it was essential that Adam and Eve join as "one" in consciousness and by that union to be fruitful and multiply within the Garden of Eden.

Unfortunately, many divine couples, many Adam and Eves, failed in that undertaking. Instead of choosing to bond together in acts of conscious love, these fallen couples regretfully chose to act individually, and out of a consciousness of self-desire. It was the choice to act out of the consciousness of self-desire that led these fallen couples to experience the knowledge of evil. The fall of these divine couples from the higher vibration of the consciousness of love to the lower vibration of the consciousness of self-desire ultimately resulted in a severance of their unity of consciousness. Without the nourishing light sustenance derived through their unified consciousness, the imperishable bodies of light worn by these divine couples, their immortal soul bodies became corrupted. With the dimming of their divine consciousness, these divine couples became subject to the control of the elemental forces within nature. By their fall into the lower order of consciousness, these divine couples joined with the other "beasts of the field," becoming creatures of nature.

As a consequence of his fall, man has become blinded to those greater realities from which he has fallen. Although we are conscious that we occupy a three-dimensional world, scientists have theorized the existence of other separate yet interwoven dimensions, parallel time frames, and even parallel universes. Still, such worlds and realities beyond our perception are also beyond our comprehension. Each level of creation—from that which man currently occupies to the most profound, yet undiscovered dimensions, parallel time frames, and universes—is pregnant with life and activity not so different from our own. The light material substances of those higher realities are simply more refined, and, of course, as one moves up the ladder, the experience of consciousness and the creative potential is profoundly greater.

In our three-dimensional reality of consciousness we create structures with matter composed of heavy steel and coarse mortar. Likewise, in order to experience our three-dimensional reality of consciousness we need to occupy a dense physical material body. However, if we were able to peek into the higher dimensional levels of consciousness, we would discover that both buildings and one's physical body are composed of malleable materials of light, color, and sound. And at the highest evolved levels of consciousness, we would see that our so-called physical bodies are composed of pure energy.

The ultimate goal of every fallen soul is to return to that perfected state of consciousness from which it has fallen, and ultimately to re-unite with the conscious love of God. For each fallen soul this is a journey home. It can and should be an exciting journey as each one of us strives to restore our magnificent and divine consciousness. While on that journey we should embrace the diversity and abundance of creation flowing all around us. Most importantly, we should recognize the inescapable fact that we are all members of a soul Family so incomprehensibly large as to have no beginning and no end. It is, in reality, a journey of love lasting an eternity.

Can we not imagine what our life experience would be like if it were not impeded by the limitations of our present physical form? We all think faster than we can act. We all create within our minds that which we find impossible to translate into form. Can we not imagine the joy of such an immortal and perpetual reality as that which we experienced in the timeless paradise of Eden? The profound question before us is how could man, so elevated by God, and having as his birth right—timeless immortality and the ability to endlessly create—have chosen so badly?

The polarities of consciousness.

The Missing Thread of Man's Divine DNA

All that has emerged out of the sea of the infinite conscious love of God, whether animate or inanimate, is born of and formed by the energy of consciousness. Man is but one of the many manifestations of conscious energy to be found within the realm of nature. However, the elevated station that man enjoys is so unique that it seems at odds with everything else that we observe within nature. There are certainly no other manifestations of conscious energy within nature equal to that of man. And although many organisms use the energy of consciousness to create their own habitats, generation after generation, spiders will continue to weave their webs the same way, birds will continue to build their nests the same way, and salmon will continue to swim upstream to spawn. The actions of such organisms, of conscious energy, found within the realm of nature are innate; they are simply a product of their DNA.

DNA is defined as the carrier of genetic information relating to the origin and functioning of living organisms and is the fundamental element of heredity. DNA research has been helpful in reaching an understanding of the complex physical nature of living organisms, including that of man. However, man is much more than that which has been discovered in the investigation of his physical DNA. Man also possesses the DNA of God.

Man emerged out of the Consciousness of God as an individual Atom of God Consciousness. As the only child of God, man bears within his matrix of consciousness certain innate attributes not possessed by any of the many other manifestations of conscious energy found within nature. Within nature it is man alone who possesses a level of consciousness that is self-aware. Only man has the capacity to declare, "I AM." Only man possesses the capacity to direct his consciousness, to choose with a considered deliberation between multiple options. Man not only possesses the ability to create incredible and wide-ranging diversity within multiple environments, he can also extend the reach of his consciousness to explore an infinite universe. More importantly, man has as an innate attribute of consciousness the ability to choose a good act over an evil act. No other living organism within the realm of nature possesses such innate characteristics of consciousness. Yet, despite such divinely endowed qualities of consciousness, man has sadly failed to pioneer discovery into his profound heritage, or to map the code of his divine DNA.

Man, having been so divinely endowed, leads to an inescapable question. Did something go wrong in the birth process of man? Was man really intended to join with the beasts of the field as a physical creature of nature? Was there possibly a combination of physical and divine DNA that was never intended to occur, at least not in the way that it has occurred? Genesis tells us that all man had to do to enjoy a timeless physical immortality in the Garden of Eden was to eat the fruit of the Tree of Life. So how did man acquire his present physical mortal body, and just how different is it from the imperishable body of dust with which man was clothed when God placed him in Eden?

The implication in Genesis is that man was clearly physical and that he ate, as, "…God commanded the man, saying, of every tree of the garden thou mayest freely eat" (Genesis 2:16). In particular, we know of two trees that bore fruit for consumption, the Tree of Life and the Tree of Knowledge. Consumption obviously implies the ingesting of something, or perhaps what is being referred to is a figurative form of consumption, such as that of action or conduct.

Does the story of Genesis provide any indication that while they resided in Eden the physical bodies of Adam and Eve looked like the physical bodies now worn by man? Although we do not know how long Adam and Eve resided in Eden before their expulsion, we do know that while in Eden, they had no children. Perhaps it is reasonable to infer that God's directive to Adam and Eve to be fruitful and to multiply was a metaphorical and not a literal expression? A directive not related to any act of physical propagation, but to their exercise of conscious dominion over "…all the earth …and over every living thing that moveth upon the earth" (Genesis 1:26). I will propose that the lack of children born to Adam and Eve while in Eden was due to the fact that their bodies, unlike those of the beasts of the field, were not capable of propagation, of producing children.

In Genesis, we are told that Eve found the fruit of the forbidden tree to be "…pleasant to the eyes…" (Genesis 3.6), and that when she and Adam ate the fruit "…the eyes of them both were opened…" (Genesis 3.7). This account of Genesis suggests a number of interesting considerations. What are we to make of the manner of sight before the fruit was eaten with that after Adam and Eve ate the fruit? Did consumption of the forbidden fruit give Adam and Eve a vision of something that they had previously not witnessed in Eden? Maybe the statement that "the eyes of them both were opened" refers to the knowledge or the experience that they gained after consuming the fruit of the Tree of Knowledge. Clearly, after consuming this fruit, Adam and Eve now knew something that they previously did not know, or that they previously had not experienced, and that they found pleasant.

Furthermore, after consuming the fruit of the Tree of Knowledge, we are told that Adam and Eve now "…knew that they [were] naked; and they sewed fig leaves together, and made themselves aprons" (Genesis 3.7). What change had occurred in their naked bodies to now cause them shame and the need to make "aprons" to cover themselves? An apron is a form of clothing tied around the waist. It does not cover the whole body. So what was it these aprons covered? These aprons covered the physical changes that had occurred in the bodies of Adam and Eve after they had consumed the fruit of the Tree of Knowledge. Their imperishable bodies of light now had sexual organs. Like the beasts of the field, like the pairs and opposites in nature, Adam and Eve now had the capacity to join in sexual union.

Although Adam and Eve had no children while residing in Eden, we do know that, once Adam and Eve left Eden, that Adam "…knew Eve…and she conceived…" (Genesis 4:1). Adam knew Eve sexually and, as with all of the pairs and opposites within nature, Eve bore offspring. Clearly, consuming the fruit of the Tree of

Knowledge caused a profound change in man's imperishable body of light, in his divine DNA. More importantly, this change led to a serious detour to occur in the evolutionary development of the consciousness of man.

Splitting the Atom of God's Consciousness

The Adam and Eve Union of Consciousness

An endless stream of the Atoms of God consciousness moving into and through the spirit/matter realms of the paradise of Eden has continued uninterrupted since that climactic union of the ineffable powers of Consciousness and Love gave birth to the energy that is the conscious love of God. There will never come a time when the Atoms of God consciousness cease emerging out of the Consciousness of God. However, while in its androgynous state, the Atom of God Consciousness lacks any degree of conscious self-awareness. Furthermore, while in the bonded state, the masculine and feminine polarities of consciousness lack the capacity to act independently of one another. Such a bonded consciousness can only and always act as the unified and perfect conscious love of God.

We all know that the experience of love is best when shared. How profound is the wisdom that created each Atom of God Consciousness as a divine couple eternally bonded together in a harmonious and dreamlike state of bliss. This is the template upon which all of creation is modeled. For Man, it is as a divine couple with the masculine polarity of consciousness embodying the Consciousness of God, and the feminine polarity of consciousness embodying the Love of God. As each Atom of God Consciousness moves through the many spirit and matter realms of consciousness, it is on a journey of evolution leading to greater and greater levels of conscious self-awareness. However, it is only through the exercise of choice that consciousness can evolve into a consciousness that is self-aware. In order to evolve into greater levels of conscious self-awareness, each Atom of God Consciousness must master all realities of spirit and matter. In order to acquire such mastery, each Atom of God Consciousness must first undergo a bifurcation or a separation of its unified masculine/feminine polarities of consciousness. Prior to this bifurcation feeling and desire always act as a perfect and harmonious union of one. In such a harmonious union, there can be no question of corruption within the bonded unity of consciousness that is the Atom of God Consciousness.

Even so, upon the bifurcation of the unified masculine/feminine polarities of consciousness, each, now as separate self-conscious entities, must choose to bond their powers of consciousness in order to be fruitful, and to multiply. The unity of the one consciousness within the Atom of God Consciousness now becomes the conscious independence of the two in the realm of nature that is the Garden of Eden. In order to dress and replenish the Garden of Eden the masculine conscious energy now resident in the man, Adam, and feminine conscious energy now resident in the woman, Eve, must bond together as one.

It is only through the proper application of the energy of the consciousness of love that each divine couple, each Adam and Eve, can evolve into higher states of conscious self-awareness. It is only through such an evolution of consciousness that a divine couple can become co-creators with God. Acquiring the wisdom to exercise the proper use of the energy of the consciousness of love is only possible within the realm of nature—the realm of duality, of pairs and opposites. Such was the path and challenge laid before each Adam and Eve upon entering the paradise of the Garden of Eden.

Adam and Eve are representative of all of the divine couples who were placed within the Garden of Eden, the numbers of which are truly beyond our comprehension. In each case, Eve, representative of the feminine polarity of consciousness, did come out of the unified consciousness of the androgynous Adam. With Eve embodying the feminine consciousness active as feeling for Adam, and Adam embodying the masculine consciousness active as desire for Eve, it was intended each would continuously seek out the other to join in blissful acts of creation. Only by the two choosing to come together as one in consciousness could Adam and Eve enjoy the creative authority vested in them within the Garden of Eden.

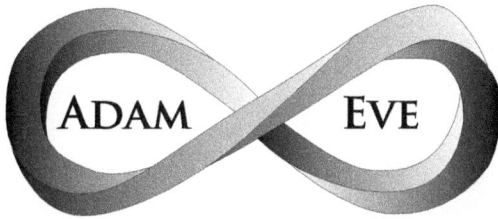

The Adam and Eve union of consciousness.

Adam and Eve and the Elemental Beings

The elemental beings are the master tailors who weave the physical clothing worn by all life forms within nature. Elemental beings lack any conscious self-awareness and, when not called upon to clothe the forms of spirit with physical matter, remain passive and inactive. Within the confines of nature, the elemental forces are called into action by the instinctual interplay between the intrinsic powers of consciousness when activated within the physical bodies of the male and female sexes. The activation of those powers of consciousness, powers that comprise the underlying component of the DNA program running within the bodies of the sexes, leads to physical sensation. The physical sensations occurring within the bodies of the sexes, and in particular the sensations arising out of sexual orgasm, awaken the elemental forces and move them to act according to their nature. The energetic union between the intrinsic powers of consciousness occurring within the physical bodies of the male and female beasts of the field assure the perpetuation of all life within nature.

Among the sexes within the Garden of Eden, the intrinsic powers contained in the masculine and feminine polarities of consciousness—of desire and feeling—are not bonded together as they are in each divine couple. Among the beasts of the field there is no unity of consciousness or, for that matter, any level of conscious self-awareness. Within nature, the powers of creation, of feeling and desire, are separated, with the power of desire residing within a male physical body and the power of feeling residing within a female physical body. The only way to ensure the propagation of each species within nature is by bringing the male and female sexes together in a physical sexual union. The coming together of the male and female sexes is spurred by elementals seeking sensations. Sensations are triggered by the power of desire within the male sex and of the power of feeling within the female sex, as each, in the appropriate season, are instinctually drawn to sexually bond with the other.

However, Adam and Eve were not numbered among the beasts of the field, among the sexes within nature. Although each divine couple, each Adam and Eve, entered the Garden of Eden as pairs, as male and female, they did so in sexless bodies. The method of creation for each Adam and Eve was not to be through a physical sexual union as occurs among the beasts of the field. Each divine couple, each Adam and Eve were to create through a union of their respective intrinsic powers of consciousness without recourse to a physical body. They did not need to physically propagate as did the male and female sexes within nature, as, after all, their bodies were imperishable, incorruptible, and immortal.

A union of the powers of consciousness by and between a divine couple leads not to physical bodily sensations, but to an experience of bliss, a state of spiritual joy and ecstasy. It is an experience that far surpasses that of any animal sexual orgasm. The experience of bliss can only arise through a union of consciousness untainted by the experience of physical bodily sensations. The experience of bliss not only nourishes and sustains the imperishable physical body worn by every Adam and Eve, it is a creative energy not controlled by or subject to the forces of nature. Nevertheless the procreation program of the sexes running within nature is designed to be automatic and self-sustaining, under the creative control and authority endowed in every Adam and Eve by their Creator, God. By merging their two independent polarities of consciousness so as to act as one unified consciousness a divine couple would not only enjoy full dominion and control over the elemental forces within nature. They would also maintain and preserve the perfect, incorruptible and immortal nature of their own physical bodies.

If a divine couple failed to bond their two polarities of consciousness as one consciousness, but instead chose to act independently and through their physical bodies, each would experience physical sensations in the same manner as those experienced by the beasts of the field. And, as with the sexes within nature, their physical bodies would also come under the control of the forces of nature. This is simply the natural evolutionary process that ensures the continued propagation and preservation of the sexes, of all of the divisions and pairs within nature.

Upon entering the Garden of Eden to continue their evolutionary journey in consciousness, each divine couple is indeed counseled not to "eat the fruit" of the Tree of Knowledge. Each is counseled to not consume the sensual energy created by the energetic interplay between desire and feeling as is experienced within the physical bodies of the male and female sexes found within nature. In other words, they are counseled to not engage in sexual union or experience sexual orgasm. Their journey into the realm of nature is solely for the purpose of acquiring knowledge of the sexes, of the pairs and opposites, sufficient to allow them to exercise creative control over all living things within the Garden of Eden.

Man's Exile from the Paradise of Eden

The Union of Adam and Eve Torn Asunder

Unfortunately, not all divine couples, not all Adam and Eves, were equal to the challenge of preserving the bonded union of their polarities of consciousness, of always acting as one in consciousness. Many divine couples took a tremendous evolutionary detour when they chose to eat the sensual 'fruit' of the Tree of Knowledge. In failing to honor and preserve their sacred marriage of consciousness, many divine couples fell to the temptation to experience the intoxicating sensations of sexual union. In so doing, they subjected themselves to the powerful and commanding elemental forces within nature, to the 'serpent' of Eden. Symbolically, the Tree of Knowledge, of good and evil, represents the knowledge that can be derived through interaction with the elemental forces within nature. Interaction with the elemental forces, when engaged in with the unified consciousness of love, leads to the acquisition of knowledge that is good. However, interaction with the elemental forces, when engaged in with a singular consciousness of self-desire, leads to the acquisition of knowledge that is evil. In choosing to experience the sensual pleasures of sexual union, the fallen divine couples chose to act out of a consciousness of self-desire. The result of that unfortunate choice was that, over time, the unity of the polarities of consciousness between Adam and Eve was torn asunder. In the absence of the unity of consciousness, these fallen divine couples lost control over their physical bodies, surrendering them to the control of the elemental forces within nature. The elemental forces, acting in accordance with their true nature, are collectively the 'serpent'. It was the improper engagement with the elemental forces, solely to satisfy a lust for physical sensation that resulted in the fall of man. Unfortunately, man's conversation with the serpent continues to this day.

I am certain that many will question how Adam in a male physical body and Eve in a female physical body would not use them for sexual activity. We need to appreciate that the physical bodies that we wear today look nothing like the original imperishable bodies of light worn by each Adam and Eve in the Garden of Eden. The physical bodies of Adam and Eve, although human in form, did not have sexual organs. Sexual organs provide the means by which all of the numerous species within nature propagate their own kind. This is a necessary function, as the physical bodies of the beasts of the field were not endowed with the eternal breath of God. Their physical bodies were not created to be immortal. Because they shared a bonded consciousness and were of one flesh, and because their bodies were imperishable, incorruptible, and immortal, Adam and Eve had no need for sexual organs.

Although the physical bodies of each divine couple were also woven together by the elemental forces, their bodies were not formed for sexual union. The program for the propagation of the male and female sexes within nature is controlled by the elemental beings. It is the elemental being who, in the appropriate season, trigger the instinctual interplay between the power of desire within the male species and of feeling within the female species. However, within every divine couple these powers of desire and feeling come together solely by a volitional act of consciousness. Adam and Eve did not enter the paradise of Eden as an outcome of a physical sexual act, but through a bifurcation, a separation of their unified masculine and feminine polarities of consciousness. It is in the non-physical union of consciousness, and not a physical sexual union, that the creative act engaged in by each Adam and Eve is distinguished from that engaged in by the sexes within nature.

The ability of every divine couple to create is through the power of the Spoken Word emanating out of their unified consciousness. This unity of consciousness allows for the manipulation of time, space, and matter and for control over all of the elemental forces within nature. Nevertheless, in order to effectively exercise authority within the Garden of Eden, it was necessary for each divine couple to acquire knowledge of nature in all of its manifestations. This undertaking included the merging of their higher consciousness with the consciousness of the lower orders in nature. By said actions the divine couples came to understand, among other things, the process of procreation among the sexes.

It was through such experiences that many divine couples became addicted to the sexual experience. This addiction became so strong that many divine couples, through the power of their consciousness, reconfigured their own physical bodies of light so as to have sexual organs. Having sexual organs then allowed them to have sexual union, not only between themselves, but also among the other divine couples as well. As is the case among the beasts of the field, there would be no discrimination among the fallen in such sexual unions. However, in so doing, and over time, these divine couples became trapped within their altered physical bodies. As a consequence, they not only suffered a corruption of their imperishable bodies of light, their immortal souls, but they also suffered a loss of their divine consciousness. With the loss of their divine consciousness they lost the ability to move freely within the many spirit/matter realms that make up the paradise of Eden.

More importantly, these fallen couples lost the ability to unite with their divine counterparts in the consciousness of love. The two were no longer able to become one in consciousness and to share the bliss of such a union of love. The result for such couples has been that they have, lifetime after lifetime, wandered throughout nature in search of their divine counterpart. This has resulted in a profound sadness within every soul as it journeys through life hoping and longing for that moment of recognition and reunion with its counterpart, its divine feminine or divine masculine consciousness. It is that longing within the heart of each of us for that feeling of wholeness and completeness that will guarantee the eventual reunion, and healing, of every such broken heart.

It is only by choosing the good of the consciousness of love over the evil of the consciousness of self-desire that each divine couple can restore the unity and perfection of their eternal marriage. The so-called command from God not to eat the fruit of the Tree of Knowledge was not a command but a caution. It was a caution to all divine couples, to all Adam and Eves as they entered the Garden of Eden, not to become intoxicated by the sensual energy within nature.

We indeed fell from grace and we did so by choice. And those of us who fell have become trapped within an illusionary world of sensual experience. Like a moth drawn to light, we are simply blinded by the glitz and glitter of the sensual experience. Let's be clear that it was not God who expelled man from the Garden of Eden. God, as infinite conscious love, is incapable of inflicting punishment. God, as infinite conscious love, allows each soul total freedom of choice. Within the exercise of choice lies the potential for self-inflicted punishment. By his bonding with the serpent within nature, man exiled himself from the paradise of Eden. The paradise of Eden is a world of timeless permanence in a state of perfect balance and harmony, operating in accordance with the universal law of conscious love. The paradise of Eden is a reality existing outside of our holographic envelope of time, space, and matter. By his fall, man corrupted not only his body, his immortal soul, but nature as well, making it a world out of balance and harmony. And it is within this corrupted holographic world of nature and not the paradise of Eden where man now finds himself. "Cursed is the ground for thy sake, in sorrow shalt thou eat of it all the days of thy life" (Genesis 3:17). "Unto Adam and to his wife did the Lord God make coats of skins, and clothed them" (Genesis 3:21). As a consequence of their fall, these divine couples are no longer clothed with their imperishable bodies of light. They are now clothed in skin, bodies of flesh subject to decay and death, and living in a temporal world whose laws mandate cycles of death and decay.

Because of our fall in consciousness, we lack access to our higher divine senses with which to see and experience the reality that is the paradise of Eden. We should not presume, simply based upon the limited experience of our five physical senses that we can never know of this reality, simply because we cannot consciously observe or experience it. To do so would be like a blind man denying the existence of the sun simply because he cannot see it. We can all take comfort in the fact that many more divine couples, many more Adam and Eves passed the test of remaining united in consciousness while walking within the Garden of Eden than failed. These immortal souls, who are our brothers and sisters, desire nothing more than to offer assistance to those of us who took the wrong path. To the degree that we remain consciously receptive, we will always find an outstretched hand.

It has only been by sinking deeper and deeper into the lower vibration of consciousness that man has taken on his current dense and coarse physical body, becoming an extension of the hierarchy that is the animal kingdom. Man remains the highest among this hierarchy simply because, and notwithstanding his fall in conscious awareness, he remains the Atom of God Consciousness clothed with the light energy of an immortal soul. In fact, if we were able to see the light of our immortal soul we would understand that we were truly looking upon the "image and likeness" of God. As man evolves and moves closer to his return to Eden, his physical body, including his sexual organs, will once again go through transformation. We all will be given a second chance to get it right.

All of us can and will ultimately be successful in our journey back to the paradise of Eden. However, we first must turn on the beacon of light that will allow each of us to clearly see our way through the world of sensual illusion. The light of the beacon is none other than the light of the consciousness of love.

The Serpent of Eden

In Genesis we are told, "... the serpent was more subtle than any beast of the field which the Lord God had made" (Genesis 3:1). Being subtle is defined as being hard to notice or see. The Serpent is not one of the "beasts of the field." The serpent is an allegorical representation of the elemental forces within nature. Like everything that emanates from the Consciousness of God, the elemental forces are composed of the energy of consciousness. The function of the elementals is to draw together the matter necessary to clothe all living things within the Garden of Eden. As the energy of consciousness, elementals do not themselves wear the clothing of physical matter. They function only through the interplay of the powers of desire and feeling occurring between the male and female sexes within nature. It is this interplay between the sexes that moves the elemental forces as the grand tailor within nature to clothe the various spirit forms of consciousness with physical matter. In that context, Genesis is telling us that the serpent was not easily recognizable; it was more subtle than all the beasts of the field.

In the story of Genesis, we are told that Eve has a conversation with the serpent regarding the various trees in Eden. She tells the serpent, "…we may eat of the fruit of the trees of the garden; but the fruit of the tree which [is] in the midst of the garden, [the Tree of Knowledge] God hath said, Ye shall not eat of it…lest ye die" (Genesis 3:2). The fruit of the Tree of Life is representative of the energy that sustains Adam and Eve's imperishable garment of light, their physical bodies. The fruit of the Tree of Knowledge is representative of the energy that sustains that which is cyclical and transitional. Adam and Eve, clothed in their imperishable bodies of light, were given dominion over all that is cyclical and transitional in Eden, to dress (clothe) and keep the Garden of Eden. Theirs was the authority to marshal and direct the elemental forces in all acts of creation occurring within Eden.

However, after Adam and Eve consumed the fruit of the Tree of Knowledge there occurred a corruption in their conscious self-awareness. The fall in their conscious awareness lead to a corruption in the light of their imperishable physical bodies, and of the balance and harmony of that which is cyclical and transitional within nature. This was all brought about through the powerful influences of the elemental forces in nature—of the serpent. The influence of these elemental forces arises from the sensations generated in the interplay between desire and feeling occurring between the sexes, the beasts of the field in nature. Adam and Eve fell because they chose to consume the sensual energy, the sensations flowing out of the physical sexual union.

"And the Lord God said unto the serpent, because thou hast done this [reduced the conscious awareness of Adam and Eve] thou [art] cursed… above every beast of the field; upon thy belly shalt thou go, and dust shalt thou eat all the days of thy life" (Genesis 3:14). Here we now see the segregation of the energy of the elemental forces and of physical matter into a separate reality where the unity between time, space, and matter are severed. This separation, this loss of unity between time, space, and matter has given us as our three-dimensional home, this temporal universe of death and decay.

We also see that, as a result of the corruption of time, space, and matter this temporal reality will be one of conflict between man and nature. "And I will put enmity between thee and the woman, and between thy seed and her seed; it shall bruise thy head, and thou shalt bruise his heel" (Genesis 3:16). The effect of the densification and segregation of this corrupted physical matter is further elaborated when God tells Adam "…cursed is the ground for thy sake; in sorrow shalt thou [eat] of it all the days of thy life" (Genesis 3:17). The ground [physical matter] is cursed because it has become corrupted within the imperishable physical bodies of Adam and Eve. By consciously altering their physical bodies so as to have sexual organs, and by consciously choosing to imitate the beasts of the field by engaging in sexual union, Adam and Eve became subservient to the laws of nature. They fell under the control of the elemental forces, the serpent within nature. And the lesser, the serpent, cannot control the greater, Adam and Eve, without corruption within the established order of creation. All that was corrupted was exiled from Eden and became our three-dimensional universe of time, space, and matter.

The Trees of Eden - You Shall Know Them by Their Fruits

As vast as the historical record of man's existence is, our knowledge and understanding of that record remains limited. This limited reservoir of knowledge has often generated heated debate among experts regarding how we should interpret what the historical record discloses. With the passage of time we find that prior opinions need to be revised as new evidence is uncovered. This triggers yet another round of heated debate on how the new evidence alters previous assumptions. Likewise, the ancient religious texts are often incomplete, contradictory and, in some cases, show evidence of alterations raising serious questions as to the reliability of their overall contents. The scientific and religious historical record is simply too incomplete to offer any definitive answer on the origin of man or his true relationship with God.

If man hopes to move closer to unraveling the mysteries of his origin he will first have to recognize that the heaven and the earth of Genesis comprise a transcendent realm of archetypal patterns formed of spirit consciousness. It will also be necessary for man to expand his understanding of the process of evolution, recognizing that it not only pertains to the transformation of matter, but also to the evolution of the archetypal patterns formed of spirit as they take on the clothing of physical matter. The two realities of spirit and matter, inseparably bonded one to the other, have evolved into the timeless realm of permanence called Eden. The experience of the multiplicity of that unified reality is dependent on each soul's level of conscious self-awareness.

Given the incomprehensible size of our universe, it is inconceivable to believe that our universe is not populated both far and wide with an infinite number of souls who bear the same relationship to God as we do. The potential diversity among such an unlimited number of souls and the degree to which each may have fallen may truly allow for a heaven in one part of the universe, a hell in another, and something in-between for the rest. The manner in which each soul rose or fell and whether it is a resident of a heaven or hell is conditional upon the fruit of that tree that each soul has chosen to eat. "Ye shall know them by their fruits" (Matthew 7:16).

Allegorically, the two trees of Genesis are representative of the two halves of the unity of consciousness; of spirit bonded with matter. The Tree of Life is symbolic of the eternal spirit that is the foundational source of the Atom of God Consciousness. The fruit of the Tree of Life embodies the elixir energy that is the conscious love of God. When consumed, the fruit of the Tree of Life sustains the imperishable physical body that houses the Atom of God Consciousness.

The Tree of Knowledge is symbolic of the creation process by which the substance of matter is drawn and magnetized around the spirit consciousness of all living things within the realm of nature. The fruit of the Tree of Knowledge embodies the sensual energy of the elemental beings. When appropriately consumed, the fruit of the Tree of Knowledge is good and insures the proper cycling and transition of matter worn by the spirit consciousness of all living things. However, when this sensual energy is consumed, not for the purpose of sustaining and nourishing the physical body that clothes the spirit forms of consciousness, but to experience sensual pleasure, then consumption of the fruit of the Tree of Knowledge is evil.

To fulfill their mandate to dress and keep the paradise of Eden, it was necessary that Adam and Eve acquire knowledge of everything within nature, within the Garden of Eden. They were to acquire knowledge by commanding the elemental forces as they engaged in various manner of creation and by interacting with the various forms of life found within Eden. The Tree of Knowledge is called the tree of good and evil, as the knowledge acquired can be good when guided by the conscious love that is of God or it can be evil when guided by the consciousness of self-desire.

For many divine couples, the knowledge acquired went beyond and understanding of the knowledge of the elemental forces and how they could best marshal those forces in acts of creation. The knowledge acquired was inappropriately used to allow them to experience sensual pleasure within their physical bodies. This action was a profound diversion from their role as creator and caretaker within the Garden of Eden. Many divine couples succumbed to the effects of sensual pleasure and by so doing, abdicated their dominion and creative authority within Eden. These Adams and Eves suffered a fall in consciousness when they became intoxicated with the feeling of sensations that they experienced when they energetically joined in sexual union with the beasts of the fields, and later when they physically joined in sexual union with each other. Over time, these fallen Adams and Eves lost control over their imperishable physical bodies and became imprisoned in mortal bodies subject to the laws of procreation and to the laws of nature.

Those who fell also lost their spiritual sight and the awareness of their original undertaking. Instead of enjoying unbounded consciousness, the fallen found themselves limited to a consciousness restrained by the physical bodily senses. After the fall into darkness, man's consciousness was not much greater than that of the beasts of the field. It is only by virtue of the conscious breath of God that man still retains in his matrix—his divine DNA—that, with the passage of time, man has been able to reach his present intellectual heights. Unfortunately, despite such advancements, man still suffers a consciousness more aligned with the beasts of the field than that of the Atom of God Consciousness. Through corruption of his divine consciousness, man has effectively created a holographic nature that, lacking in the fullness of the consciousness of love, is a realm of impermanence, death, and decay. There are but two choices for each evolving divine couple, each Adam and Eve, when standing before the Tree of Knowledge. They can choose to always act as one, unified in the higher consciousness of love, or the two can choose to act separately, each in the lower consciousness of self-desire.

The failure to remain faithful to the marriage between the masculine and feminine polarities of consciousness was what has become characterized as the 'fall of man'. The so-called original sin was man's deviation from the original plan to further the evolution of his unified Atom of God Consciousness, the result of which bound him to a world of death and decay. Choice was and still is the privilege of each divine couple. There has always been the choice to choose the good of the consciousness of love and return to the immortal state or to continue to choose the evil of the consciousness of self-desire and to remain imprisoned within this holographic world of nature.

Each Atom of God Consciousness imprisoned within an animal body provided by nature must reclaim its authority over the elemental forces if it is ever to restore its physical body to the imperishable state. For the majority of us, the powerful drug of physical sensual pleasure continues to hinder that effort. We not only lack control over our own bodies, we lack any awareness that control over our bodies is in fact in the hands of the elemental forces within nature. And we are ignorant of the fact that the most powerful elemental force controlling our bodies is that of sex and the desire for sexual union. Regretfully, the majority of us continue to choose such sensual pleasures over immortality.

Since that fateful moment of our collective fall, man has again grown in conscious self-awareness: the inner light is returning and many are once again preparing to submit to the test of the right and proper use of the energy of creation, the consciousness of love. We can accelerate the completion of that test if we are bold and courageous enough to change the old paradigm of how we view this mortal experience of life. Within each heart vibrates a remembrance of the paradise called Eden. It will be through the proper exercise of choice in the use of the energy of creation that man will eventually succeed and joyously return to Eden.

Eve Alone Did Not Cause the Fall of Man

Genesis suggests that it was the woman, Eve, who first succumbed to the temptation to consume the forbidden fruit and then led the man, Adam, astray. However, a more careful reading reveals that Adam was with Eve when she first ate and shared the food with him. "And when the woman saw that the tree [was]... pleasant to the eyes, and a tree to be desired... she took of the fruit thereof, and did eat, and gave also unto her husband with her; and he did eat" (Genesis 3:6).

"After consuming the forbidden fruit, Adam and the woman [Eve] now knew that they were naked; and they sewed fig leaves together; and made themselves aprons" (Genesis 3:7). From Genesis 2:25, we know that, prior to eating the forbidden fruit, Adam and Eve knew that they were naked but they were not ashamed. What had changed in their bodies that would cause them such shame? Their shame was that their physical bodies now had sexual organs. It becomes apparent that now having sex organs like the beasts of the field presented a major problem for Adam and Eve.

"Unto the woman he [the Lord] said...in sorrow thou shalt bring forth children; and thy desire [shall be] to the husband, and he shall rule over thee" (Genesis 3:16). Although this sounds like an angry God placing woman in a subservient role to man, what is actually being acknowledged is the relationship between the feminine and masculine polarities of consciousness. The essence or power contained within the feminine polarity of consciousness is expressed as feeling'. The essence or power contained within the masculine consciousness is expressed as 'desire'.

It is the role of feminine consciousness, when active as feeling, to create beauty within form. Feminine consciousness is always the initiator in the creative process—the "mother of all living" (Genesis 3:20). It is the role of masculine consciousness, when active as desire, to give the force of life to that which has been formed by its counterpart. The feminine power of feeling seeks union with the masculine power of desire in order to complete her creative act. Therefore, it is the masculine consciousness expressed as the power of desire that rules over [thee] the feminine consciousness expressed as feeling.

"And Unto Adam he [the Lord] said...cursed [is] the ground for thy sake; in sorrow shalt thou eat [of] it all the days of thy life; for out of it wast thou taken; for dust thou [art,] and unto dust shalt thou return" (Genesis 3:17-19). "And Unto Adam also and to his wife did the Lord God make coats of skins, and clothed them. (Genesis 3:21). No longer are the physical bodies of Adam and Eve made of imperishable light. They have corrupted their immortal souls, their physical bodies of light, with the consumption of the forbidden fruit. In so doing Adam and Eve engaged in the improper use of the energy of creation, the energy of the consciousness of love. As a consequence, Adam and Eve were relegated to live among the beasts of the field in perishable bodies of flesh. Their physical bodies, no longer being composed of the substance of light, but of flesh, became subject to the cyclical and transitional forces within nature.

Because of the severance in the unity of their consciousness, it was further necessary for Adam and Eve to leave the paradise Garden of Eden. "...the Lord God said, Behold, the man is become as one of us, to know good and evil..." (Genesis 3:22). To know of good and evil is, among other things, to know of and to experience sexual union. By choosing to imitate the sexes within nature in acts of sexual union, Adam and Eve defiled their polarities of consciousness. This caused Adam and Eve to fall into a lower level of conscious awareness. Their lower level of consciousness is now closer to that of the beasts of the field. "Therefore the Lord God sent him forth from the Garden in Eden, to till the ground from whence he was taken [the realm of nature]" (Genesis 3.23). However, the realm of nature into which the fallen divine couples were exiled was not like the perfect and harmonious realm of nature within Eden. These divine couples found themselves confined within an artificial and holographic reality, a grand illusion fashioned by their own corrupted consciousness.

It is regrettable that Eve, as the representative of the feminine, has been so maligned throughout history as the cause for the fall of humanity. Although Adam and Eve entered the paradise of Eden as two, they were intended to always act as one in the right and proper use of the energy of creation. Eve could not have acted alone to eat the forbidden fruit. It was necessary for Adam, as the active principle of desire, to empower Eve as the passive principle of feeling, with action. Nevertheless, feeling always precedes desire and accordingly, Eve, as feeling, can be viewed as the initiator of the action that led to the fall.

However, Adam, as the active principle of desire, sealed the action. The reality is that neither could have acted alone. The Adams and Eves who fell failed in the command that the two shall always act as one in consciousness sustained by the fruit of the Tree of Life. Adam and Eve, failed to preserve their union, but were "torn asunder" when they each willing chose to consume the sensual energy within nature, the fruit of the Tree of Knowledge. Their volitional choice was as an act of selfish desire (evil). Instead of choosing to preserve their blissful conscious union of love (good), they chose, in imitation of the beasts of the field, to experience physical sexual union. Those of us who fell have been paying the unfortunate consequences ever since.

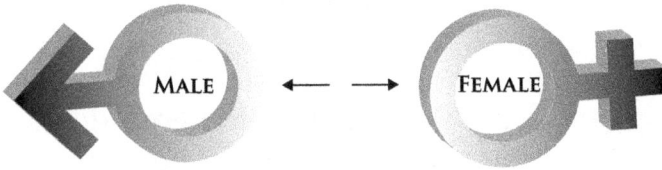

The union of Adam and Eve torn asunder.

PART V

Adam and Eve's Addiction to the Forbidden Fruit

Eating the Forbidden Fruit Leads to Sensual Addiction

Within the paradise Garden of Eden, each divine couple, each Adam and Eve, were endowed with unlimited creative authority. However, sexual union was not the intended manner by which divine couples were to engage in the act of creation. Sexual union as a method of creation was designed so as to allow for the continuing propagation of the lower orders of creation, of the beasts of the field. Within nature, sexual union is the only method of creation available to those lacking in the wholeness of a unified consciousness.

Instead, all divine couples were to emulate the creative union from out of which they had emerged, that being the union of consciousness and love. Each divine couple was to create through the harmonious union of their powerful forces of consciousness. In so doing they would enjoy the full and unchallenged authority over the lesser forces of nature. However, many divine couples fell to the temptation to emulate the beasts of the field and to experience sexual union. They became so enthralled with this activity that they used their powers of consciousness to alter their bodies of light so as to have sexual organs and the capacity to engage in sexual union.

In taking on a distinctly sexual form, these divine couples acquired a gender identity. Over time, this gender identity created a perception of separation and individuality that ultimately led to a severance of the unity of consciousness shared by these divine couples. This severance between the polarities of consciousness further led to a feeling of isolation among the fallen. Feelings of individuality eventually lead to comparisons, which gives birth to ego. The competition among egos leads to envy and jealousy. The outcome of such a downward spiral is conflict, which gives rise to pain and suffering.

So long as man sees himself as an individual ego in competition with others, he will fail to see the forest for the trees, or the conscious love of God within all men. Without breaking this pattern of thought, man will continue to relegate himself to live in a world dominated by his insatiable desire for the fleeting sensual experience. Man can and must break the domination of the forces of nature over his physical body and free himself from the insatiable lust for the sensual experience.

There are but two choices facing each of us. We can choose the good found in the right and proper use of the energy of creation, the consciousness of love. Or we can choose the evil found in the energy of disharmony, the consciousness of self-desire. One choice will result in the restoration of the eternal marriage between every divine couple, every Adam, as the true masculine, and every Eve, as the true feminine. The other will result in our continued confinement to this holographic virtual reality, a reality where in ignorance the true feminine and the true masculine are locked in perpetual conflict fueled by self-desire.

To be successful in making the right choice we first must acknowledge that the evil actions we witness by, between, and among men exist not by decree of God, but solely by the choice of man. Earth has become the classroom in which man, in the exercise of choice, must learn of the creative power of love as that which is good, and the destructive power of self-desire as that which is evil. The reality of love is harmony. The reality of self-desire is dis-ease and disharmony. Until each of us masters this universal law, we will fail to achieve redemption. Admittedly, the path back to Eden is a path not easily traveled. It is a testament to the courage of all who consciously take on this challenge. Not only must we brace ourselves against the evil tendencies existing within the world at large, but we must also fight the powerful elemental addictions gripping our own physical bodies. We are all familiar with the obvious and often crippling addictions of alcohol, drugs, and sex. But to not limit himself to these many avenues of sensual pleasure, man, aided by his technological talents, is continually exploring ways to create other means of mind and body stimulation. Over time, man's unrelenting search for and consumption of sensual stimulation further dampens and depresses his higher divine consciousness.

Now, as a species within nature, we struggle with a consciousness that is in conflict. On one hand, we are controlled by the lower instinctual consciousness that we share with the beasts of the field. From that level of consciousness, we seek out those primal needs for food, sexual gratification, and dominance over other members of our species. Yet we are also influenced by the higher consciousness of love residing within our heart. It is the consciousness of the Atom of God Consciousness. At that level of consciousness, we seek the peaceful harmony that can only be found in a brotherhood of love. Within the confines of our three-dimensional reality, the model for that unity of brotherhood and love is found in the nuclear family where members are bonded together in a commonality of purpose and relationship. To his credit, man has made attempts to expand the family model of brotherhood and love within a broader framework of nation states. However, to date, he has failed to bind those diverse nation states into a truly global family united in a commonality of purpose, brotherhood, and love.

That failure is due to man's inability to access his higher divine consciousness. Lacking such access leaves man to function from the more limited consciousness found within the confines of nature. It is a consciousness dominated and controlled by an unrelenting stream of sensations being filtered through man's physical bodily sensors. Our insatiable desire to experience mind and body stimulation blinds us to an awareness of our higher divine consciousness and restricts us to the belief that we are nothing more than the physical bodies we occupy. For many, the philosophy of life is to eat, drink, and be merry, for tomorrow you shall die and the grand party of mind and body stimulation will end. And for many, the belief is that when it is over, it is really over, with no heaven or hell—just oblivion. We first must acknowledge and then confront our addiction to the sensual life experience if we ever hope to awaken to the greater reality of our conscious immortality. Many divine couples did faithfully follow the blueprint of the plan of their evolution and now enjoy all the fruits of life in the paradise of Eden. Unfortunately, those of us reading this did not choose as wisely. We chose the party over paradise.

There is hope, however, and as you read this take heart in the fact that we have never left the paradise of Eden, but we have succumbed to the drug of the sensual experience to such a degree that we are unaware of that greater reality to which we remain connected. We are lost in a world of sensually created illusions, a virtual holographic reality of our own creation. As a result, we remain unconscious of the brotherhood of souls of which we are members. In our diminished state of consciousness, we are unaware of those successful divine couples residing within the paradise of Eden who are desperately trying to assist us out of our drug-induced state and back to an awareness of our true reality as immortals.

As man journeys back to Eden, he will eventually restore the balance and harmony of his higher divine consciousness and step out of this holographic reality he has created for himself. The "nature reality" we now occupy is not the nature we enjoyed in the paradise Garden of Eden. The Garden of Eden is a realm in perfect balance and harmony where the weather is always comfortable, the animals are always docile, and the vegetation is always edible. By the corruption of his divine consciousness man has effectively short-circuited and perverted the flow of sensual energy that feeds and sustains all life within nature. By the perversion of his divine consciousness, man has corrupted nature, turning it into a violent and broken realm, not just on his planet, but throughout the universe as well.

Let's for a moment consider the disharmony generated by the thoughts of the seven billion humans beings currently residing on Earth. As each of us seeks to satisfy an insatiable desire for mind and body stimulation and as each of us engages in the means necessary to satisfy those insatiable desires, we are figuratively seven billion uncontrolled explosions of greed, lust, anger, and violence. The effect of this collective violence not only traumatizes each one of us, but also disrupts the natural harmony and balance within nature. The result is nothing short of man's warring not only against one another but against nature as well.

The power contained within each immortal soul is the limitless power of the Consciousness of God. Albert Einstein, a twentieth-century physicist, understood the metaphysics of God, recognizing that man is more than the sum parts of his physical body.

E = mc2 is an equation formulated by Einstein, in which E represents units of energy, m represents units of mass, and c2 is the speed of light squared, or multiplied by itself. Because the speed of light is a very large number and is multiplied by itself, this equation points out how a small amount of matter contains a very large amount of energy. Consider for a moment the energy contained in the Atom of God Consciousness (E), clothed in the physical matter of an immortal soul (m), and squared by the light of a limitless conscious self-awareness (c2). Einstein's equation suggests that it is perhaps most fortunate that man has not yet discovered the key to unlocking the tremendous power of the energy contained within his higher divine consciousness. It is a power not only capable of creating universes but destroying them as well.

Until we move beyond our addiction to the physical sensual experience, the powerful light of the higher divine consciousness within each of us will remain hidden. We all have the same choice. We can make a conscious decision to return to the paradise of Eden or to remain self-confined and warring within a nature made violent by our corrupted consciousness. And let us all be clear—nature is not the bad guy. It was man who imprinted upon the tapestry of nature his sexual body. Nature, now in providing man with his physical body, is merely acting as it was intended to act. The role of nature is to preserve that within its realm through the use of the conscious light bestowed upon it. Man, by his fall, has initiated a war between light and darkness, man and nature. So long as man continues to fall to the sensual addiction he will live in darkness, denying himself the guiding light of his higher divine consciousness. Only when man recognizes physical sensations for what they are will he recognize the illusion they create—the glitz and glamor of life. Only by awakening to that greater reality will the cravings for the sensual experience lose their power, and only then will light overcome darkness.

Until we understand that we have surrendered control over our bodies to elemental forces we will remain slaves to those forces. Man's five physical senses are the means by which he draws into his body a limitless stream of sensations. It is through the physical senses that man feeds his addictions. As long as we remain bound solely to our physical senses, we will remain imprisoned in these mortal bodies. As long as we think, aided only by the physical senses and what we believe they present as a wholesome synthesis of the life experience, we will remain imprisoned in these mortal bodies. Our sense-based passive thinking only fuels our dependency on the sensual experience. We must engage our higher divine consciousness in the right use of thinking if we are to ever break free of these mortal physical bodies.

At present, the catalyst for most thinking originates within the experiences derived through the physical senses. The catalyst for all thinking should originate within our higher divine consciousness through a manner of thinking characterized as inspired imagination. We can all remember that, as children, we frequently engaged in episodes of imaginative thinking. It is thinking not attached to the physical senses or to sensual stimulation. When engaged in imaginative thinking we are disconnected from our physical senses and detached from our surroundings.

Inspired imagination is the process of thinking that is engaged in by the immortal soul. It is our doorway to the realm of light from whence we all came and to which we all long to return. Unfortunately, such creative thinking has always been seen as inferior to the sense-based passive thinking that is primarily observational as opposed to initiative. Initiative thinking by inspired imagination can lead us out of the world of darkness and illusion. However, this will not happen if we do not begin to engage in the right use of our higher divine consciousness.

The Greatest Addiction of Them All

Among the beasts of the field, sexual activity is primarily tied to instinct and season. Notwithstanding their lack of conscious self-awareness, it can be assumed that the male and female sexes of the lower order also enjoy the sexual experience. In fact, there is evidence derived from studies of animal sexual behavior that strongly suggests that even in animals, sexual activity creates pleasurable and desirable sensations, not painful ones. Yet for the beasts of the field the urge for sexual union is more a component of their nature-endowed instincts, a function of the procreation program running within their physical DNA.

However, for man the urge for sexual union is far greater than what can be associated with a nature-endowed instinct to insure the propagation of the human species. For man, the urge for sexual union surpasses the functioning of any instinctual procreation program running within his physical DNA. For the fallen immortal, the physical sexual union has become the doorway through which each must enter this holographic three-dimensional reality. "I will greatly multiply thy sorrow and thy conception; in sorrow thou shalt bring forth children" (Genesis 3:16). However, human sexual activity has evolved into a function seemingly devoid of any sense of sacred purpose. Man fails to understand the sacred role sexual union plays in forming the bridge between this temporal world and the timeless realm of permanence that is the paradise of Eden. Man has taken sexual union beyond its primary function as a doorway through which an immortal consciousness can enter the temporal classroom of earth to pursue a curriculum of redemption. Instead, he has relegated this profound purpose of sexual union to a backseat while giving pre-eminence to all manner of sexual activity as a form of play and entertainment.

What man does not understand is that sexual orgasm is but a faint echo of the blissful ecstasy experienced in the union of the polarities of consciousness when engaged in by a divine couple. When a divine couple consumes the energy found in animal sexual orgasm, they corrupt the balance and harmony of the higher vibratory energy within their immortal light bodies. The highest energy power available to man is the light energy flowing from out of the right and proper use of the energy of creation, the energy of the consciousness of love. Man wastes this powerful creative energy in uncontrolled sexual activity simply for the purpose of experiencing sensual pleasure. Man must learn to temper his unrestrained desire for the consumption of sexual orgasmic energy if he hopes to return to that blissful and ecstatic union of consciousness enjoyed by divine couples. To the degree that he can be successful, man will slowly cease being the human beast of the field and again become the immortal human within nature.

Success will only be achieved when we come to truly understand the consciousness of love. The word sex is defined as the instinct or attraction drawing one sex toward another. The definition of sex does not include any reference to the consciousness of love. Man's misuse of the vibratory power of the light energy of creation in the unabated consumption of elemental animal sexual energy was the primary cause of his fall and exile from Eden. No matter how great the effort to elevate and enshrine sexual activity, man will not and cannot redeem himself through the very activity that brought about his fall. We need not swing the pendulum to a total denial of sex. However, we do need to better understand the role of sex while in exile. More importantly, we need to acquire a sacred respect for the creative role of sex and how to make it representative of the union between the divine masculine and the divine feminine.

At present, we find ourselves far removed from any understanding of the sacred creative role to be found within the human sexual union. Through the sexual union man literally can reach across the bridge connecting two worlds and choose to become a co-creator with the conscious love of God. Man can, by such an act of conscious self-awareness within the act of sexual union, thereby choose to provide a physical vehicle for another divine, although fallen, consciousness. Unfortunately, however, man fails to see the sacred act in the sexual act.

On the other hand, within the context of man's biology and psychology, much has been written on the subject of human sexuality. We have defined what constitutes good sex and what constitutes sex that is not so good. The male and female erogenous zones have been thoroughly mapped and various techniques have been devised for maximizing responses within those zones. We are no longer content to let our bodies naturally experience the sensations derived through sexual activity. Instead, we have put the best minds of science to the task of developing pills and creams designed to increase the size of sexual organs and the intensity of orgasms. A variety of birth control options are also available to ensure that pregnancy does not interfere with the opportunity to enjoy the sensual pleasures of sexual activity on demand. Man's addiction to unrestrained sexual activity was the reason for his fall and the loss of divine consciousness. Surprisingly, it has been the one addiction that man has been more than willing to suffer during his long exile from Eden.

History has shown that, as man has marched through one civilization after another, he has been preoccupied with sexual activity. We continue to be overly fixated on each other's sexual organs. Our fascination with sex is reinforced by constantly being told of the importance of sex in our daily lives. We are told that those who regularly engage in sexual activity live longer, healthier, and happier lives than those who do not. Sex is so predominant in our lives that the use of sexual content out-paces and out-performs all other advertising models in the marketing of services and products. Sexually charged advertising is designed to convince us that sexual appeal is essential for a full and satisfying life. We rush to purchase an unending stream of products guaranteed to enhance our quotient of sexual appeal. Sex appeal has become the essential criteria in choosing the clothing we wear, the autos we drive, and even the associations we form.

We are programmed to believe that without sexual appeal we cannot be popular, successful, or attractive to the opposite sex. Sexual energy pervades all mediums and arenas of activity. It is so central an activity that we are continually exposed to the sexual scorecards of public figures, from rock stars and movie screen idols to our political and social leaders. In fact, we seem to derive a prurient satisfaction from the exposure of the sex lives of such notables. No other addiction is as pervasive and all-consuming as that of sex. There are some who would argue that our views on sex are still antiquated and in need of greater liberation. Yet by enjoying greater sexual freedom, we have lost the ability to create truly committed and sustaining heartfelt relationships.

Unfortunately, man's fascination with sex is not just about the joy of sex. Thriving worldwide industries exist on the sexual exploitation and sexual slavery of women and children. Such industries feed the most debased nature of man's sexual addiction. Man's unrestrained sexual activity has also fostered a plague of sexually transmitted diseases, some of which are painfully incurable. Not to be deterred, man has developed vaccines and antibiotics to deal with such diseases. And in an effort to avoid such diseases altogether, man has advocated a program of safe sex practices. It therefore becomes possible to play with fire without getting burned.

This is not simply a case of too much sex interfering with healthy, loving relationships. The addiction is so extreme as to constitute a weapon of abuse. Excessive sexual activity has become as destructive to the mind and body as any drug addiction. Sexual activity does not feed the Adam and Eve immortal consciousness within each of us, but our out-of-control carnal animal nature. Man was never intended to become part of the animal kingdom, and least of all to imitate the beasts of the field as to sexual activity. Yet man has gone beyond simply imitating the beasts of the field where sex is tied to seasons of propagation. Man has taken sex beyond its creative function and turned it into sport. The painful reality that we must face is that, as a child of God endowed with immortality, man chooses a physical life of sexual excess. And worse yet, man makes this choice despite the trauma caused to so many others in seeking to satisfy an insatiable appetite for personal pleasure, domination, and control.

Unrestrained sexual activity forms yet another underpinning of the current paradigm imprisoning man in coats of skin and delaying the restoration of his divine consciousness and triumphant return to Eden. Until we learn that sex is the tie that binds us to nature and blinds us to our higher divine consciousness, we will continue to walk in darkness. Man will eventually overcome his addiction to consuming the forbidden fruit, which does nothing more than feed a consciousness of self-desire. As he awakens in conscious awareness, man will choose instead to once again consume the fruit of the Tree of Life—the fruit that sustains the consciousness of love. In choosing good over evil man will restore the blissful union of consciousness between the masculine and the feminine, which is the hallmark of the sacred marriage between every Adam and Eve.

Sex, Love, and Relationship

Why do so many relationships fail? In part it is because we equate the sensuality of the sexual experience with love. We have come to believe that sexual activity and love are inseparable companions. In reality, sex has not a thing to do with love. Sex, however, has everything to do with biology and hormonal chemistry. In an effort to legitimize our passion for unlimited and unrestrained sex, we have fashioned a social creed that maintains that sex is an essential and necessary component of a successful relationship. With such a belief system, the experience of unlimited and unrestrained sex will most often always trump the experience of love.

Too often we first jump into sex; as for love…well, time will tell whether he or she is the right one. Unfortunately, most of us tend to get lost in the romance of sexual attraction and the excitement of the sexual experience and give little thought to the romance found in the consciousness of love. While lost in the romance of sexual attraction, we confuse the sensations of sex with love. The result of such confusion often leads to disappointment and, in many cases, a broken heart.

We have all been down the road of confusing the romance of sexual attractiveness with the romance of love. Unlike the consciousness of love, physical and sexual attractiveness fade over time. How many of us thought that we had found Mr. Right or Ms. Wonderful, only to discover six months later that such was not the case. After a brief recovery period, we are back on our feet, but unfortunately none the wiser, as we will repeat the mistake of identifying the romance of sexual attractiveness and the sensual sexual experience with love. I am not advocating that we suppress our animal nature, and least of all that we should stop having sex. We are perhaps eons from breaking those bonds of nature. However, we must learn to distinguish those transient and, by comparison, superficial physical sense experiences from that which is truly profound and enriches our lives in ways that words often fail to adequately capture. Contrary to what many believe, that something is not 'good sex'. It is the consciousness of love found only in a union of the masculine and the feminine polarities of consciousness. True love occurs only within such a union of consciousness.

For most of us, love is most often a case of how I feel, my expectations, and what I want out of a relationship. We seem to never get beyond the personalization of love and move on to a true conscious exchange of love. Admittedly, it all starts with physical attraction. For that fact, we have the elementals of nature to thank. They are simply doing their job and doing it very well. Remember, it is how they ensure the continuing propagation of all life within their domain. Yet there is much more taking place when boys and girls meet. It is not physical attraction alone that makes you want to spend every waking moment with your newfound love, or has you walking on air and feeling that the heavens have opened above your head.

Yes, to a small degree, physical attraction and physical sensations can trigger such feelings. But not to the degree as does the union of feeling and desire that, when experienced, not within one's erogenous zone but within one's heart, results in a powerful and electrifying conscious experience of love. The heart is the center within each of us wherein resides the polarities of consciousness. It is within the hearts of women where the sweet and gentle essence of the consciousness of feeling resides. It is within the heart of men where the quiet yet powerful essence of the consciousness of desire resides. Love is born in the conscious union of those two powers and the experience born of such a union is not sensual, but blissful. Love is not born within a sexual orgasmic experience. All that is born within the experience of sexual activity are stimulating bodily sensations.

It is the experience of the consciousness of love that triggers a powerful recognition between two souls. It is the consciousness of love that draws the true feminine and the true masculine together, creating a genuine and blissful intimacy within the heart. We all come into this virtual reality with a remembrance of what a conscious love between the masculine and the feminine feels like. After all, each of us started out as a divine couple, an Adam and Eve. As a divine couple we enjoyed the experience of the blissful union born out of the shared intimacy of those electrifying powers of consciousness, of desire and of feeling.

It is only in the balanced and harmonious union of the two, of the feminine consciousness expressed as feeling and masculine consciousness expressed as desire that true love flourishes. Unfortunately, within man desire and feeling no longer work in a balanced or harmonious way, but each is out to satisfy itself. The fact, not yet fully appreciated, is that love is an experience of consciousness and not an experience born through physical stimulation of the body. Love is that conscious unifying energy that binds all within creation. Without love, there would be no heaven and earth, no paradise of Eden, or, for that matter, God.

We are all an Adam or an Eve seeking the opportunity to experience true love. And there is no greater experience of love than for those divine couples who, on their long journey back to Eden, are fortunate once again to find themselves reunited within nature. At the higher conscious soul level, we each come into this virtual reality committed to seizing the opportunity to once again come together in a profound conscious reunion. The means of recognition between divine couples can be found in simple things, such as the inner light reflected in a person's eyes or in the radiance of a smile. Unfortunately, in too many cases, before the recognition is fully made by the consciousness residing within the heart, we become preoccupied with the romance of the sensual sexual experience. The enjoyments of sex then overlay the deeper recognition of that conscious love we each carry within our hearts. The result is, too often, the creation of a weak relationship prone to difficulties and an inability to create an enduring intimate relationship of the heart.

We fail to recognize that love is not about 'me', but about 'us'. Love works best when it is shared, when there is a complete conscious surrender of self-desire with no expectation of receiving anything in return. When partners meet each other in such a state of surrender, the only experience possible for each is an all-encompassing conscious love; an enduring relationship of the heart. It is only by creating such heart relationships that we can put sex back into its proper place. When we achieve that level of conscious self-awareness, we will begin to treat sex more as a spiritual act leading to the creation of a vehicle to house an Atom of God Consciousness. When we move away from the sensual experience of sex and toward the sacred experience of conscious love, we will have earned the opportunity we previously forfeited. We will once again have the opportunity as divine couples to come together in a union of conscious love. In such a union we will find the restoration and wholeness of our unified consciousness. Until man's attitude towards sex matures he will continue to suffer the consequences of this addiction and remain bonded to the temporal and transitory. As in all recovery programs, the first step is to acknowledge the addiction.

The Consciousness of Love Must Overcome the Power of Sex

We need not get bogged down in a discussion of whether sex is something good or something bad. We need only understand that the dynamic behind the urge for sex is simply nature's way of insuring the continuing propagation of all of the species within its realm. It is an inescapable fact that, as long as we continue to live in these animal bodies—bodies created and sustained by nature—we will continue to engage in sexual activity. However, the question is: will we continue to throw ourselves into unrestrained sexual activity or will we awaken our higher divine consciousness and define the role of sex for a soul striving to reclaim its immortality?

Since our exile from Eden, we have drifted further from an understanding of our inherent divine consciousness while continuing to feed on a diet of forbidden fruits. We have taken sexual activity beyond the design of nature and expanded it into a form of sensual entertainment. In so doing, we have forsaken the opportunity to bring the sacredness of the consciousness of love into the creative process tied to human sexuality. As long as we choose to travel the road of sexual pleasure, we will fail to recognize the consciousness of love as our path back to Eden.

Many will argue that a man and woman are brought closer together in sexual activity and that enhancing the sensual pleasures of sex can only help to increase such bonding. As previously stated, sex is simply a matter of biology and hormonal chemistry. No matter how much we try to elevate the role and importance of sex, the fact is that, unlike the shared experience of love, the experience of sex is a wholly selfish act. We delude ourselves when we contend that we engage in sex as a means of demonstrating love for our partner, or that we engage in sex to give the gift of pleasure to our partner. In fact, it is the pleasure that we stimulate in our partner that stimulates our own sexual pleasure. In sex, we lose ourselves, not in an act of conscious love, but in the experience of physical sensual pleasure.

Man has turned the sexual act into a pleasure cult as addictive as the chemical drugs that we deem dangerous to our bodies and minds. Our addiction to unrestrained sexual activity is fueled by the portrayal of explicit sexual subject matter across a broad spectrum of media for the sole purpose of stimulating sexual desire and erotic satisfaction. By comparison, the voice of conscious love and its role in the masculine/feminine relationship is heard as but a faint and distant echo. For those who are serious about returning to the paradise of Eden, it is now time to place the search for the consciousness of love above the search for the sensual pleasures of sex.

Until we recognize that love is an experience of consciousness, we will continue to link love to our experience with sexual activity. Unfortunately, we have married sex to love and turned it into the romance of sensual sexual love. The result has been to relegate the experience of love to a physical experience of the senses, when in truth it is wholly an experience occurring within the consciousness of the heart. When we relegate love to an experience of the senses, it then becomes a singular experience with the focus on oneself. The experience of love then becomes not one of selfless love, but one of satisfying self-desire. So long as our individual self-desire is being fed the sensual fruit of sex, then love is a grand experience. Once our self-desire is no longer being fed, then it is time to move on, once again, in search of that one true love. However, without recognizing that love is truly a union of consciousness and not that of the spasmodic sexual union between two bodies, such a search will always prove futile.

It is the union of the feminine and of the masculine powers of consciousness anchored in the heart that is the source and wellspring of a truly intimate and sustaining love. For love to flourish, the two must become one in consciousness. The failure of the masculine and the feminine powers, of the two becoming one in consciousness, results in a broken heart. We feel the loss of love in our hearts and it is a feeling that has nothing to do with sex.

A Marriage Made in Heaven

The template of each Atom of God Consciousness is patterned on that bonded union of Consciousness and Love, expressed as the infinite conscious love of God. Each Atom of God Consciousness, although containing both a masculine and feminine polarity of consciousness (God created he him; male and female created he them) is nevertheless without animal sexual identity. As long as each Atom of God Consciousness remains in the androgynous state, these powers of consciousness remain bonded together in a blissful state of perfect love, as, after all, each Atom of God Consciousness is a perfect expression of the conscious love of God.

To recapitulate: upon entering the paradise of Eden, the two polarities of consciousness were separated to stand independent of one another. The feminine polarity of consciousness, the essence of which is feeling, was embodied in the woman Eve as the feminine/mother principle. It is the feminine power of feeling that is responsible for creating the beauty of form within matter. The masculine polarity of consciousness, the essence of which is desire, was embodied in the man Adam as the masculine/father principle. It is the power of the feminine that always initiates creation by providing the physical vessel for life. It is the power of the masculine that always instills life into that which the feminine has formed with matter. Such acts of creation are accomplished through a union of consciousness, not through a physical sexual union. This is truly a case of the divine marriage, of the feminine and the masculine principles, coming together as eternal companions to multiply, to be fruitful, and to create throughout the many timeless realities that comprise the paradise of Eden.

With our conscious self-awareness restrained by our five physical senses, we struggle with the concept of creation occurring not through a physical sexual union but through a union of consciousness. Although physical in the material sense, the bodies of Adam and Eve were not formed to allow them to join in a sexual union or to create through a physical sexual act. The method of creation for Adam and Eve was solely through a union of consciousness. Adam and Eve entered the Garden of Eden enjoying the unlimited freedom to create throughout the many spirit/matter realms of Eden, clothed in the spirit/matter dress of their choosing. Adam and Eve entered the Garden of Eden as co-creators with God.

Unfortunately, far too many divine couples did not choose wisely in the exercise of the unlimited freedom granted to them. Fascinated by the sexual merging of the male and female sexes within nature, many chose to "eat the sensual fruit" offered by nature. Having the power of consciousness to do so, they merged with the many beasts of the field in order to experience sexual union. Although initially without sexual organs, the desire to experience sexual union with their own bodies resulted in their use of the elemental forces of nature to transform their bodies in order to have sexual organs. Instead of remaining faithful in consciousness with their own divine counterpart, many divine couples not only entered into sexual unions with each other, but also promiscuously consorted with other divine couples. The outcome of this flagrant sexual activity resulted in tearing asunder the unity of consciousness shared by these many divine couples.

As a consequence of engaging in sexual unions, those who fell eventually suffered a loss of the conscious awareness of their immortal state. Over time, they also lost the ability to separate themselves from the powerful elemental forces within nature. As a further consequence, they became separated from their divine counterpart; compelled to wander throughout the realm of nature, lost to one another. Since that consequential moment, each fallen Adam and Eve has been searching for their divine counterparts. In time, these separated couples will find themselves together once again. Each Adam and Eve will be given another opportunity to restore the blissful union of their conscious love. We all have had many such opportunities. However, the pull of the sensual and the sexual has continued to blind us to the eternal rewards to be found in that sacred union of conscious love.

Within each beating heart, there is a faint remembrance of that blissful union once shared. Within each divine couple, there resonates a unique sound of love. No two divine couples are alike in the sound of love resonating within their hearts. That remembrance creates a longing in each of us to meet Mr. or Ms. Right, our one true love. It is that coming together and the experience of that enduring love that we are all seeking. Regrettably, we are all constantly falling in and out of relationships. Such relationships start off fine but do not prove sustainable. We are not fulfilled, do not feel complete, and intuitively we know that something is missing. That something is the love that can only be found in union with our divine counterpart.

Unfortunately, the distractions of the sensual world and the unequal level of advancement among divine couples hinder the sought-for recognition. We cannot all expect to meet up with our divine counterpart in the first relationship that we may choose to form with another. However, in our journey toward that sought-after reunion, we need to rethink our view of what it means to be feminine and what it means to be masculine and of the proper relationship between the two.

Love Is a Shared Experience

We will better understand the power of love when we recognize that love is an experience of consciousness awakened within the heart. Regrettably, within this virtual reality we have created for ourselves we identify that which is feminine and that which is masculine as qualities of the sexes relating to physical characteristics and sexual behaviors. Throughout this book, I have identified the Atom of God Consciousness as the bonded union between the true masculine and the true feminine. I do so not because they are sexual in nature. The true masculine and the true feminine are powers of consciousness, sexless and without gender. So let's strive to move beyond mere physical characteristics and behaviors and into a better understanding of the true essence and power of the feminine and the masculine.

The Powerful Essence of the Feminine

All women desire to be seen as feminine. However, for many, femininity has become synonymous with the sensuality of sexual appeal. As a result, we have come to view femininity as an externalized quality enhanced by the way a woman dresses, the style of her hair, the perfume she wears, and a perfect 10 figure. However, true femininity is an inner quality that is neither created nor enhanced by external factors; it is the power of the feminine consciousness being expressed as feeling and not the power of sensuality that is the hallmark of true femininity.

Unquestionably, men are attracted to the beauty of the female form, particularly when it has been adorned to provide that alluring sensual and sexual appeal. Men gladly feed upon the fruit of the sensual energy offered by women. Nevertheless, it is truly the quality of the feminine when expressed as feeling that really attracts and holds the attention of men. Men desire the essence of feeling emanating from the feminine and intuitively understand that it is in a bonded union with the feminine essence of feeling where they will find a true intimacy and that inner experience of happiness.

With the focus so strongly placed on the female form it is difficult to describe that uniquely mystical quality of femininity, of the consciousness of Eve within all women. Femininity is a quality that transcends the perceived measure of external physical beauty woven by the elemental forces of nature. The feminine consciousness when expressed as feeling is most evident in the silent yet gentle strength of surrender to the masculine. In surrendering to the masculine, the feminine is surrendering that which it wishes to form and create to that which has the power to give life to its creations. It is in this union of the two, of feminine feeling and masculine desire, that all creation is possible. Femininity is the soft and gentle feeling of love being given to another. It is a selflessness born out of the power of the true feminine.

Unfortunately, men (often in a state of self-absorption) see the act of surrender by women as a victory on their part. They fail to recognize the strength that is behind the gift of love. It is a strength nevertheless founded upon a heartfelt belief that, in their act of surrender, they also will find the gift of love. Unfortunately, in the pursuit of sensual pleasure, men often do not give but simply take.

The Powerful Essence of the Masculine

In like manner, men desire to be seen as masculine. As with femininity, masculinity is often equated with exterior physical sensual qualities. Tall, dark, and handsome will always get the attention. However, masculinity is an inner quality that is neither created nor enhanced by external factors. Masculinity is the essence of the masculine consciousness when being expressed as desire.

Unquestionably, women are attracted to the strength of the male form, and particularly when it has been enhanced to provide that alluring and sensual sexual appeal. Women gladly feed upon the fruit of the sensual energy offered by men. However, it is the quality of the masculine, when expressed as desire for conscious union with the feminine that attracts and holds the attention of women. Women long for that essence of desire emanating from the masculine, and intuitively understand that it is in a bonded union with the masculine essence of desire where they will find a true intimacy and the inner experience of happiness.

With the focus so strongly place on outward physical appearances, it is difficult to describe that unique quality of masculinity, of the consciousness of Adam within all men. Masculinity is a quality that transcends the perceived measure of external physical attractiveness woven by the elemental forces of nature. The consciousness of the masculine, when expressed as desire, is most evident in the surrender of its power to give life to the feminine. Masculinity is that strong yet gentle desire of love being given to another. It is a selflessness born out of the power of the true masculine.

Too often women, in a state of self-absorption, see the surrender of men as a victory on their part. They fail to recognize the strength that is behind the gift of love. It is a strength nevertheless founded upon a heartfelt belief that, in the act of surrender, they also will find the gift of love. Unfortunately, in the pursuit of sensual pleasure, women often do not give but simply take.

And the Two Shall Be As One

Each of us must awaken to the reality of the conscious love of God residing within our hearts. We draw closer to such understanding by recognizing that love is an act of consciousness unrelated to any contact between two physical bodies. Contact between two physical bodies simply leads to the creation of physical sensations so powerful that the sweet call of love fades into a distant echo. Love is born when the feminine, expressed as feeling for the masculine, and the masculine, expressed as desire for the feminine, become united as one in the consciousness of love. It will only be through such an awakening that all divine couples, each Adam as the ideal man and each Eve as the ideal woman, can realize a restoration of their divine marriage and a return to the paradise of Eden.

PART VI

The Journey Home

The Journey Home Will Not Be Easy

Man lives in a world of pain and suffering as a direct consequence of his fall in conscious self-awareness. This world of
pain and suffering is an illusion but appears real because our flawed
consciousness makes it appear so. That which we believe to be reality
is but an unconscious dream, and a bad one at that. In this dream
state we are asleep and therefore blinded to the true relationship between the masculine and the feminine and their respective powers of
consciousness. Our blindness prevents us from seeing that happiness
can only be found in the coequal and harmonious union of those two
ineffable powers.

It is this apparent separation between the masculine and feminine powers of consciousness that causes so much pain and suffering. Believing that we are separate, we wander through a dreamlike
virtual reality, alone and confused over the proper relationship between the genders. We will continue to unnecessarily suffer so long
as we see the relationship between the genders as being primarily a
marriage of the sexes instead of a marriage of and within the energy
of consciousness. The inescapable reality is that despite man's fall
each divine couple, each Adam and Eve, continue to remain inseparably bonded in the wholeness of their unified consciousness. In our
fallen dreamlike state we are just unaware of that wholeness, a unity
that can never be broken as each divine couple, each Adam and Eve,
are eternally bonded one to the other.

All creation is simply the progressive and evolutionary expansion of the energy of consciousness. The creative act engaged in by divine couples occurs through a joining together of their respective polarities of consciousness. This energetic union of consciousness is the only manner by which a divine couple can create. The indissoluble union between the polarities of consciousness ensures that the evolution of consciousness will never cease and that creation will always be fruitful and endlessly multiplied.

Even so, the failure of the two polarities of consciousness to act as one results in the inability to create through an act of consciousness. This failure of consciousness can only result in the creation of a flawed and discordant reality. The severance in the bonded unity of consciousness among the fallen has resulted in the creation of a reality woven together out of vast amounts of weakened and unsustainable thoughts. The outcome of such a severance in consciousness is most often an unrelenting stream of sensual thoughts fueling an insatiable desire for unrestrained sensual experiences. All of these sensual thoughts, desires, and experiences come together to create the illusion of a cohesive life experience. Through the misuse of the creative energy of consciousness, the fallen have imprisoned themselves within the walls of their physical senses.

So long as we remain locked behind the walls of our physical senses we will be bound to our perishable physical bodies. Ignorant of our conscious immortality we will continue to suffer cycles of death and decay within these coats of skin while endlessly trying to satisfy an insatiable appetite for sensual stimulation. So long as we remain blinded by the sensual experiences derived through our physical senses we will continue to confine ourselves within a nature fashioned by our weakened consciousness.

There is a way out. We can unlock the door and escape this three-dimensional holographic program. The key to our escape from the prison of sensuality is to be found in the right use of the energy of consciousness. In order to find the key we must seek a greater understanding of the reality from which we have all emerged. That reality is the conscious love of God. In search of that greater understanding, a reliance solely on our collective experiences derived through our five physical senses will hinder more than help. We are, first and foremost, an individuation of the conscious love of God.

Within the holographic dimensional reality of consciousness that we have created for ourselves, our sensually based thoughts are weak, fleeting, and incoherent. As a consequence, we fail to recognize that both the thinker, as well as the activity of thinking, exists outside of this artificially created three-dimensional reality—both are to be found within the immeasurable breath that is each Atom of God Consciousness. Our diminished conscious self-awareness makes creative thought more often the exception than the rule.

We all struggle to create a coherent, understandable, and sustainable reality with our thoughts. In a world made up of so many different perceived realities, we each see ourselves as unique among the many. We most often find it difficult to embrace the thoughts of others who, because of the insular and confused nature of their thoughts, see and experience a reality different from our own. The result is often one of intense frustration as we try to persuade one another that the reality we see is the true reality and that all other perceptions are flawed. Reliance solely upon our physical senses further limits our ability to witness any reality not accessible through those senses. As a result, we deny the existence of realities existing beyond those revealed through the physical senses. More importantly, we fail to recognize our greater reality as the Atom of God Consciousness, as a son and daughter born of the conscious love of God.

In order to move beyond such restraints it is first necessary to acknowledge the limits of searching for answers solely through the medium of the physical senses. We need to understand that the key to exploration of the as-yet-unknown lies within the thinker of thoughts and that the medium wherein both are found is consciousness. In order to unlock the mysteries of the universe we will need to enter the expanse of consciousness, and we will have to do so aided with more than just the physical senses. We need to activate our God-endowed higher senses of consciousness. In doing so, we will discover that consciousness is the energy that binds together all physical matter and all of that within infinite realities of consciousness. We will discover that the reality we call the universe is in fact composed of both spirit and matter, each manifesting in multidimensional states of consciousness.

In this effort, science will have to overcome its bias that only in seeing is believing possible. Over and again history has shown that what science has unequivocally and categorically claimed to be fact has to later be acknowledged as false when new means of discovery makes such an acknowledgment unavoidable. The Earth is no longer flat, the sun does not revolve around the Earth, and the universe is much larger than the galaxy we occupy. Science needs to acknowledge its handicaps in that regard and to employ senses not traditionally associated with its observations of time, space, and matter if it ever hopes to solve the riddle of a first cause or a unifying principle connecting all levels of matter within all dimensions of this universe.

We ceased to be amazed by the capacity of the human brain to act as a coordinating center for the processing of vast amounts of sensory data. There are some who believe that the brain is the primary organ responsible for the experience of consciousness and thought. Yet, despite extensive research, science has been unable to definitively answer the question of whether consciousness and thought are in fact nothing more than by-products of the chemical and electrical activity of the brain, or whether there is something beyond mere biology and chemistry at play. In other words, can there be consciousness and a thinker of thoughts without an organic animal brain? If the answer is no, then perhaps man is nothing more than a highly-evolved biogenic artificial intelligence machine similar to that exceptional android Data of the fictional Starship the USS Enterprise. However, even if that is the case, we are still confronted with the question of first cause, as even Data had a creator.

Even if we were compelled to conclude that we are nothing more than highly evolved biogenic artificial intelligence machines, something of an intelligence or consciousness factor would, of necessity, have preceded creation of the machine. That is, of course, unless we believe that such a highly evolved biogenic intelligence machine as man simply self-evolved out of a random confluence of energy transformations. But, if that were the case, why would such an evolutionary transformation of energy stop at man? The animal species demonstrate an evolution of consciousness greater than that evidenced within the plant species, and man demonstrates an even greater level than that evidenced within the animal species. In the estimation of science it has been over 13 billion years since the universe was born. Are we to assume that the evolutionary transformation of consciousness, as seen within the biogenic intelligence machine that is man, has reached its maximum evolutionary capacity?

For those of us who have followed the Starship Enterprise on its mission of exploration, we have witnessed the efforts of the android Data to become more like a human. Yet, Data was never able to become more than the accumulated sum of the informational data he acquired in his interactions with his human shipmates. Data could not demonstrate originality outside the operational parameters of his computer program. His positronic brain was not capable of spontaneous creative thinking. Even Data's experience of emotions was an analytical exercise, a further computation of data on how humans act. In experiencing emotions, Data did not acquire wisdom or form the ability to emotionally empathize with others. Data lacked a capacity for self-conscious awareness. Unlike Data, man is endowed with the consciousness of his Creator. Man possesses a self-conscious awareness and that awareness is not predicated upon any accumulated data stored in his biogenic brain. In other words, man has the capacity to think beyond the operational parameters of his biogenic brain processor. To believe otherwise would lead to an unchallenged conclusion that we are all truly nothing more than human looking informational machines—that we are all Datas.

For man, consciousness is much more than that which results from an endless stream of sensory input translated through the organ of the brain. Consciousness is experienced not within the organ of the brain, but within the mind of man. The brain is an organ of the body and a receptor of sensual data. The mind is an organ of consciousness and synthesizer of all sensory data filtered through the brain, or such other data as may be assessable through the functioning of our higher senses. This synthesizing by the mind creates a logical interconnection of data that results in what is called intelligence. Intelligence then becomes the building material for the creation of edifices of thought. These edifices of thought then come together to form what we identify as reality. At present, the mind of man is preoccupied with the processing of an unending flow of physical sensual data. Most often the result is a stream of thoughts lacking in coherence or the potency to create uplifting and enduring edifices.

Unlike the prized accumulation of intellectual data, imagination is relegated to the realm of fantasy—as that which is not real. Imagination is defined as the faculty of forming mental images of something that is not present to the physical senses. As a consequence, we tell our children that daydreaming about things that are not real or engaging in a visionary form of creation through the use of imagination are a waste of time. We teach our children that if they are to succeed in life they must get their heads out of the clouds of creative thinking and plant their feet firmly within the stream of sensory data filtering through the organ of the brain. However, we have it backwards. We teach our children to live in a world of sensory-fuelled illusions when we should instruct them to live in a reality in which the self-directed use of the energy of consciousness allows them to move beyond the mere accumulation of sense data and to become creators.

The realm of consciousness cannot be explained solely by an examination of the sensory data experienced within the organ of the brain. Such an undertaking, while remaining embedded within the construct of a reality created through external data filtered only though the five senses, is a futile endeavor. One cannot identify an experience if one is the experience. That is why science's refusal to court a spirit of consciousness as a component of matter will leave itself handicapped in its search for a full and complete understanding of our temporal world reality and our place and purpose within it. Science continues to search for evidence of a unifying principle connecting everything within the field of time and space, when the evidence, and in fact the means of discovery, are to be found outside of that experience. As long as science denies that anything experientially real exists outside of the temporal field, it limits itself to an impossible task and a continuing cycle of failure.

Theories of a non-temporal reality have always persisted in man's developmental history. Since antiquity man has examined, theorized, and speculated about the temporal world and his place within it. After millennia spent in said undertaking, and despite having gained considerable knowledge of the mechanics of the temporal world, man still searches for that elusive fact, that undivided wholeness that underlies all reality, that one all-unifying quantum principle by or from out of which all things have emerged. Yet he does so without embracing that essential component without which he would be unable to engage in such a search—the energy of consciousness. Man needs to awaken to the reality that the thinker and his thoughts, although undeniably present within an envelope of time, space, and matter, also exist independently of and outside of that reality. And that this other reality in which the thinker and his thoughts exist is a reality composed of the energy of consciousness. Only by embracing such a theory can man ever hope to build a bridge between the seen and unseen and recognize the inescapable truth that consciousness is the foundational platform for all realities.

We Need to Think as an Atom of God Consciousness

Man needs to awaken to the realization that as a thinker he is also a creator. It has been through the collectivity of human thought spawned over eons of time that man has created this holographic universe program in which he has confined himself. It is a creation fashioned, not out of the proper use of the light energy of consciousness, but out of a collective and corrupted consciousness preoccupied with the desire to satisfy an insatiable appetite for physical stimulation. Man no longer thinks like an immortal being. Man no longer creates through a union of the masculine and feminine powers of consciousness. Instead, man creates through a thought process prompted and dominated by an endless stream of sensations surging through the receptors of his physical body.

For man to break from the control that the elemental forces exercise over his physical body he must overcome his sense-based passive mode of thinking and in its place engage in a cosmologically based active mode of thinking. When in the paradise of Eden we created through the power of consciousness. We must rediscover the power contained within the energy of consciousness and its proper use in creation. Then we will understand that creation is only possible in the marriage of the masculine and feminine powers of consciousness, and only then in the creative act of the two becoming one in consciousness. It is the offspring of this fruitful union of consciousness that manifests as the many multi-layered realities of spirit consciousness clothed in matter.

We can no longer experience these many multi-layered realities of consciousness because we have yielded our creative authority to the elemental forces within nature. We have done so in exchange for their providing us with an endless stream of stimulating sensations to excite our physical bodies. We have become so drugged with the effects of these sensual bodily stimulants that, even while awake, we are in fact asleep to our reality as an immortal consciousness. So long as we remain in that sensually drugged and fallen state of consciousness we will continue to live our lives in a virtual non-reality fashioned out of our collective mass illusions. Man needs to wean himself off of the conscious-numbing drug of the sensual experience, exit the virtual non-reality, and open his eyes to the wondrous vistas that comprise the many timeless spirit/matter realities of consciousness; realities of which he is, has been, and always will remain an inseparable and indispensable part.

We are all on a journey to restore our high state of conscious awareness. Because we are presently under the control of the elemental forces our thoughts are predominately focused on sex, food, power, and numerous other objects of self-desire. This pattern of sensually induced thought has resulted in the creation of an artificial edifice imprisonment that acts as a restraint on man's ability to recognize his true identity as an immortal being. Man has put himself in a very small box and fear of the unknown keeps him confined there. Better the consumption of the many sensual drugs offered by nature, even if they provide only fleeting satisfaction, than to set sail on the sea of consciousness into the great unknown. It is time for man to stop living in the shadows created by his sense-based passive mode of thinking. Man needs to restore his divine consciousness and re-establish the marriage between the masculine and feminine powers of consciousness. In so doing we will build a bridge that will allow us to once again freely move between the many realms of spirit and matter consciousness.

To achieve this goal, we will need to recognize that thinking does not originate in the organ of the brain, but in the heart and seat of our divine consciousness. The heart, as man's spiritual center, is the true brain of immortal man. The cerebellum exists to help the heart brain—a non-physical brain—process what the thinker determines to create. All creation occurs through the unity of the consciousness of love occurring within the marriage between the masculine and feminine powers of consciousness. However, so long as we continue to look for answers by confining our search within the envelope of our three-dimensional reality, we will never find the spiritual center of man—the source of consciousness and the doorway connecting the many realms of spirit and matter consciousness.

For most of us, the catalyst for thinking is found in the responses generated through physical sensations. Like Pavlov's dog, we are trained through our bodily sensors to seek out pleasure and to avoid pain. This creates a mode of passive thinking triggered by the processing of data through the physical senses. A stream of sensory data activates a neuro-synaptic process within the brain that generates a series of images joined together in a more or less uniform pattern. We call this neuro-synaptic process 'thinking' and the uniform patterns of the images arising from it 'thoughts'. Our thinking occurs not as a function of our higher consciousness, but as a result of a never-ending stream of sensual experiences provided to us by nature.

There are many who have temporarily crossed the threshold of our three-dimensional reality of conscious awareness and have found themselves in an awe-inspiring place. Many have reported interactions and conversations with beings clearly of a higher consciousness. Such conversations are reported as occurring not with the use of vocal cords, but through an effortlessly fluid exchange of thoughts. These beings of higher consciousness have been described as radiating a purity of light and warmth of love not otherwise witnessed or experienced within our three-dimensional reality of consciousness. Because of the otherworldly quality of these crossings, they have been characterized as near-death experiences. Notwithstanding that in a near-death experience there is a temporary separation of consciousness from the physical sensors of the body, those who have reported such experiences have also reported the survival of their conscious self-awareness. Many, in fact, have written extensively of their experiences. All of these individuals relate that what they experienced occurred in some reality clearly distinguishable from that of their normal three-dimensional experience of conscious awareness. Despite the numerous reported accounts of such crossings into other states of conscious awareness, and despite their shared commonality, which crosses all cultural lines, science has argued that such dimensional crossings have no basis in reality. Science contends that such reported experiences are nothing more than a fascinating dream initiated by chemical activity occurring within the brain as a result of a trauma to the physical body.

It is an established fact that we all dream when asleep. And some of our dreams are indeed fascinating. However, how many of us within our own immediate family, let alone among the greater population at large, report a shared commonality of nightly dream content or experience? Not until man breaks through such self-imposed restraints will his thinking, as a function of consciousness and not as a function of mere biology, become more apparent. For the past century, quantum physicists have intensified their search for that one element unifying everything within the universe. To date they have been unable to solve that mystery solely by examination of the biology or mechanics of matter.

Physicists could greatly advance their search for this unifying principle by recognizing that consciousness is in fact energy as much as it is a state, condition, or process associated with comprehension. There have been a number of academic scientific studies on the energy of consciousness with surprising results. One ground-breaking explorer in the study of consciousness was Robert Monroe (1915-1995). Monroe developed what he termed hemispheric synchronization or brainwave synchronization, a process that employed sound to synchronize the two hemispheres of one's brain. I like to view the right hemisphere of the brain, the assumed seat of intuition and creativity, as emblematic of the feminine polarity of consciousness, and the left hemisphere of the brain, the assumed seat of logical and analytical certainty, as emblematic of the masculine polarity of consciousness. It was by marrying the two hemispheres of the brain thorough certain combinations of sound frequencies that Monroe discovered he could evoke in test subjects expanded or altered states of conscious self-awareness.

Another interesting area of research saw the development of a method of seeing using a form of perception not associated with the five physical senses. This method of extra-sensory perception is known as remote viewing (RV). In remote viewing dimensional parameters of time and space become irrelevant and are actually transcended. The subject or target of an exercise in remote viewing can be physically located in an adjoining room or thousands of miles away. It is an exercise occurring within the boundless regions of consciousness and is unaided by any of the physical sense receptors. Notwithstanding that test results in remote viewing proved statistically impressive, mainstream science has not found such research worthy of their consideration.

There has also been some limited research on whether human consciousness survives death. Can we talk to the dead? The many reported near-death experiences suggest that we can. How many times have we heard of an individual claiming to have received a warning from a deceased loved one about an impending event that prevented an injury or death? Such warnings are also called premonitions, which are defined as an advance warning about a future event, or a strong feeling without an apparent basis that something is in fact going to happen. Might a premonition be the energy of consciousness being transmitted by a being of higher consciousness across dimensional boundaries, much like radio wave transmissions? Unfortunately, such phenomena fall outside of the standard matrix of scientific study, and, as a consequence, research on the phenomena of consciousness does not yet receive the same level of respectability or credibility as the more traditional areas of scientific inquiry.

Creation Is an Act of Inspired Imagination

It is an interesting dichotomy. Man avows an unquestionable belief in an unseen Supreme Being, yet finds it difficult to otherwise give credence to that which he cannot verify by one of his five physical senses. Perhaps man's belief in a Supreme Being is nothing more than an entrainment of the mass consciousness originating out of primitive man's fear of the normal occurrences within nature. In the absence of a scientific explanation, the violent displays of nature as witnessed by primitive man could certainly be attributed to the unseen hand of a powerful being. In fact, modern man still trembles in fear at the awesome sights and sounds of nature.

Even so, the fear-based thinking and the superstition that it spawns do not form the predicates for scientific or spiritual research. For science, any phenomena that cannot be explained with the aid of the five physical senses or with the aid of technology will languish in the nebulous arena of theory. Science sees man and the universe as nothing more than intricate physical organisms, the secrets of which can be discerned with proper investigation and experimentation. Through the knowledge so gained, science believes that it defines a world without recourse to a divine presence or power. Science is content to examine the artwork but has chosen to ignore the artist. It is time for science to meet the artist and to discover that behind all manifestation are artists whose tools of creation are not to be found in sense-based passive thinking. The tools of creation used by such artists are found within the unified powers of consciousness actively expressed as imagination and inspiration.

It is within the union of consciousness between Adam and Eve with the feminine principle of Eve active as imagination and the masculine principle of Adam active as inspiration that the creative process unfolds. The feminine consciousness, when active as imagination, initiates the creative process by conceiving, forming, and projecting a thought. It is then that the masculine consciousness, acting as the light of inspiration, completes the creative cycle by giving the power of life to that which the creative imagination of the feminine has conceived. Without inspiration, imagination remains just a dream, a wish seeking fulfillment. True thinking originates not in the physical brain but in the seat of conscious love located within the heart of each of us. The heart is the true brain of immortal man. The cerebellum exists to aid the heart brain, the center where the consciousness of love resides, while it is within the temporal realm. It is only by passing through the heart and experiencing the marriage between the feminine and masculine powers of consciousness that man can give birth to and properly endow his thoughts with life. In the absence of such a marriage of consciousness, man's thoughts are nothing more than empty shadows and vapid phantoms.

All creation occurs through an act of consciousness, an act of conscious love. It is how every Atom of God Consciousness as an embodied immortal soul creates. Imaginatively inspired thinking is not conditioned upon the existence of a physical organ, but is an activity occurring within the infinite expanse of the conscious love that we call God. It is an activity not bounded or restrained by any parameters of time, space or matter. On occasion, all of us have lost ourselves in episodes of imaginatively inspired thinking to which we have given expression through art, poetry, dance, or song. And, although entertaining, we have been taught to believe that engaging in imaginatively inspired thinking is just pretending, making believe. As children, we are chastised for wasting time in useless and unproductive daydreaming. We are counselled to get our heads out of the clouds of fantasy and our feet back on the ground of reality. As a result, we lose that inherent and natural ability to think and thereby to create. In its place we engage in an external stimuli-based, passive, reactive method of thinking, which, by comparison, is frustrating and most often leads to sterile, uninspired, and insipid thinking.

By discounting imaginative thinking in the learning process we also handicap inspiration or that ability to infuse life into the creations of imagination. Instead of recognizing the creative power contained within imaginative thought when infused with inspiration, we employ our thought process to simply acquire and retain massive amounts of existing data, just like the Star Trek character Data. On the other hand, inspiration gives life to imaginative thinking. The result is the potential for endless and varied forms of creation. Time and again we read a book, see a movie, look at a painting, and are taken to an uncommon and moving experience. That uncommon and moving experience is the offspring of the marriage between imagination and inspiration.

The experience of imaginatively inspired thinking leaves us with an ability to immediately understand something without labored reasoning. It takes us beyond the simple awareness of self to an experience of something greater. More importantly, we begin to recognize that what we create through the use of imaginatively inspired thinking are creations worthy of continued existence. And, in some cases, such creations earn the distinguished status of becoming an enduring classic work of art.

Occasionally we are gifted with the presence of an individual who demonstrates the potential of imaginatively inspired thinking. One such individual was Randy Pausch (October 23, 1960 – July 25, 2008). Mr. Pausch was a professor of Computer Science and Human Computer Interaction at Carnegie Mellon University. In 2006, Professor Pausch was diagnosed with pancreatic cancer. In 2007, and facing the approaching end of his journey, he decided to give one last lecture to his students. The lecture was entitled The Last Lecture: Really Achieving Your Childhood Dreams. Professor Pausch gave this lecture in front of a live audience at Carnegie Mellon University. The lecture was recorded and eventually circled the globe, literally touching and inspiring the hearts of millions of people. Professor Pausch did not lecture his students about living the sensual life to the fullest; he talked to them about giving life to their imagination and making their dreams a reality. Professor Pausch told his students to reach beyond their grasp and, by his own example he showed them that they could. Professor Pausch spoke as a kindred soul. He awakened within our hearts a realization that we are all part of something truly eternal, a remembrance of that bond of conscious love that we all share as immortal beings. The feeling of love was so profound; we they did not want to let him go. However, a few short months after his lecture, Professor Pausch succumbed to his illness.

Unfortunately, and despite such a profound demonstration of the creative potential of the consciousness of love that resides within all of us, we eventually fall back into our customary sense-based passive mode of thinking. However, imagine what the world would be like if each of us thought like Professor Pausch, as a timeless immortal, capable of turning our dreams—our imaginations—into reality. Our dreams—our imaginations—when inspired, become our reality. However, to become reality, we have to believe that our dreams are something real. Professor Pausch's philosophy of life demonstrated that he retained the ability to think as an immortal while on his brief journey in this temporal realm. We all should follow in the footsteps of such a man.

The Path to Redemption

We are much more than our physical bodies or the sum of our life experiences. We can change the reality we live in by overcoming our addiction to the sensual life and becoming more aware of our immortal conscious self. Collectively, we must draw the lesson plan that, if faithfully followed, will ensure our successful return to the paradise of Eden.

First, man must, at all levels of human experience, whether of a social, religious, or political nature, embrace the reality that this temporal life experience is an offshoot of the greater timeless and permanent reality of Eden. Furthermore, we must realize that despite our fall we remain an integral part of that permanent reality. As humanity collectively matures in its understanding of the detour that it took into nature, it will gain a clearer understanding of the scope of the journey that lies ahead. Such an understanding will form the underpinnings for a new paradigm of thought that can facilitate the successful restoration of man's higher divine consciousness and his successful return to the timeless paradise of Eden.

Second, each of us needs to respect the unique individuality and freedom of choice with which we were all endowed. Progress will only be made when we all stop trying to live the lives of others and focus on how better to live our own. We are all too vested in what others do. This excessive investment in the lives of others often leads to envy, anger, and hatred. The greatest pain and suffering within this temporal matrix is caused by such human failings.

Third, we must recognize that fear is no man's friend. From the individual to the largest political, social, or religious entity, there is too great an effort to control others through the use of fear. Fear-based control comes in many forms. Emotional rejection, verbal degradation, public humiliation, control over job or financial security, threats of and actual physical assault are some of the tools of fear we all employ to effect control over others. The use of fear is a negation of the divine within man and puts us on par with members of the animal kingdom. The jungle mentality of 'every man for himself' must end. We must move beyond the principle that advocates for survival of the dominant. We each are, in fact, our brother's keeper, mutually bound together by a God code of love, compassion, and charity. In the greater reality of our collective human experience, we all should hold to the philosophy that as goes one of us so must go all of us. Let's not forget that we are all on this journey back to Eden together, and all of us for the same unfortunate reason. Before our fall into this virtual reality, we were bonded together in a true brotherhood of love, each one of us having been created by the same Conscious Love that we call God.

With an understanding of our true reality as sons and daughters of God, we can and should support one another on the journey home. Admittedly, some will be content to believe that this temporal reality is all that there is, so why not enjoy it to the fullest? Such friends may try our patience. However, in this holographic classroom of Earth, the upperclassmen have an obligation to offer patient assistance to the underclassmen. It is certain that those who have successfully completed the game called Life and who have returned home triumphant nevertheless remain bonded to us in the brotherhood of love. It is also certain that they continue to assist those of us who are still stranded in this virtual reality. Of course, we all know that to be the fact and we call those assisting hands guardian angels.

In fact, such help begins before we enter this dimensional envelope. As in any undertaking where success is the goal, there is detailed planning. All contingencies are evaluated, after which an itinerary and an agenda are established. To do otherwise is to invite chaos and disappointment. There are presently seven billion souls on Earth, not to mention the infinite number residing elsewhere within this dimensional envelope that we call the universe. Just imagine the potential chaos and disappointment that would exist if all of those seven billion lives began without the benefit of a detailed life plan. The chaos and disappointment that any of us now experience is simply the result of our individual failure to follow the agenda—the rules of the game—adopted prior to our entry into this virtual reality. The success of any life agenda comes down to the proper exercise of choice. Unfortunately, the right choice is often made difficult by the flood of illusions created by our unabated sensual desires. It is a flood that overwhelms our higher conscious self-awareness. We are simply blinded by the glitz, the glamor, and the allure of the sensual within nature. As long as we continue to consume the forbidden fruit, the sensual energy offered by the serpent, the elemental forces within nature, we will continue to live in darkness, blinded to the light of our immortal soul.

Bad choices hinder the successful advancement of our individual lesson plan and ensure our continued imprisonment in a mortal body. Good choices lead to the attainment of wisdom, the successful completion of our lesson plan, and the restoration of our imperishable bodies of light. Whatever the outcome of the lesson plan may be it is always preceded by choices freely made. There can be no blame cast upon another for the chaos or disappointment of a life lived. At any point in our life journey each one of us has the ability to reflect upon how we are living our life and whether it is being lived in the consciousness of love or in the consciousness of self-desire.

In fact, I believe that it is in that act of reflection when made as the end of life approaches that gives rise to our fear of death. It is a fear born out of an inescapable assessment that our life was, in fact, not well lived. We reflect on the pain that we caused others, which at the time we justified for one reason or another. We reflect on the many opportunities missed and the lack of any significant accomplishments within the time that we had been allotted. Most significantly, we regret the failure of not taking the time to repair torn relationships. How many have wished for the opportunity to make things right in the dimming light of life's approaching end? Would death not be less fearful and traumatic if we but embraced the reality of our conscious immortality, of the journey of redemption we eagerly set upon, accepting that there may be failures along the way, yet knowing that, despite such failures, we would be given unlimited opportunities to succeed?

As immortal beings, we will always be given the opportunity to right the wrongs committed and to restore harmony where we have created disharmony. It does take immense courage for each of us to keep coming back into the game of life, particularly when the wrongs that must be righted may be substantial. Often, people ask why bad things happen to good people. In reality there are no victims. People who commit bad acts, as despicable as they may be, are our teachers and facilitators in helping us to right our own wrongs that may be long, if not mercifully, forgotten.

The Lesson Plan

As Atoms of God consciousness we were all vested with dominion over the paradise of Eden. In furtherance of the evolution of our conscious self-awareness, we were to enter the realm of nature as immortal and divine couples for the purpose of acquiring knowledge in the proper use of the elemental forces in nature. We were to acquire this knowledge of nature without misusing the knowledge acquired. The proper use of the knowledge acquired is assured when its use is guided by the consciousness of love residing within the heart of each divine couple.

Actions flowing from the consciousness of love lead to harmony and to that which is good. Improper use of the knowledge of nature leads to a state of disharmony and to that which is evil. By his misuse of the knowledge of nature man violated the perfect order, balance, and harmony of the consciousness of love residing within his heart, and for that sin he suffered exile from the paradise of Eden. Man alone can and must restore the balance and harmony that he has disturbed.

Restoration of harmony and balance is only possible by the right use of the energy of creation, the energy of the consciousness of love. We all need to understand that it is not God who inflicts punishment upon man for transgressions against the natural order. It is man, who in the exercise of the freedom of choice, chooses to violate the law of love. The violation of the law of love sets in motion the inescapable law of restoration. It is a law that makes every man his own incorruptible judge. The law of restoration decrees that each of us shall suffer the consequences of our choices and of the imbalances that we have created until we have restored the balance and harmony of love displaced by those choices. It is a perfect, just, and inescapable law.

The road leading to redemption requires that each of us regain mastery over the elemental forces within nature. By mastering the elemental forces we will regain mastery over our physical bodies. Mastery can only be achieved by the restoration of the balance and harmony between the masculine and feminine polarities of consciousness. Until such mastery is achieved, man's physical body will continue to suffer decay and death. Such mastery will remain elusive until each of us awakens to the consciousness of love that resides within our hearts and, by right choice, declines to consume the sensual fruit of the Tree of Knowledge. We are all like moths drawn to the lure of the light of the sensual, which is nothing more than an illusion leading to death. Man, through his five senses, is addicted to the sensual experience that he runs to embrace but that he finds is never fully satisfying. So we keep reaching for more, injecting our senses with the sensual stimulants provided by nature, further dulling our conscious self-awareness.

It will only be by changing the paradigm and creating a spiritually grounded science of life that recognizes that the origin of man and the universe is to be found in that greater reality existing outside of our envelope of time, space, and matter. Such a paradigm needs to accept as a basic premise that each man is endowed with an immortal physical body of light called the soul, and that this physical body of light is as real outside of time and space as is the physical body we wear within the envelope of time and space. Additionally, we need to come to the realization that our envelope of time, space, and matter is a corruption of the timeless and permanent realm of nature within the paradise of Eden, and that it exists solely as a result of man's fall, of his corruption of the energy of creation.

Such a paradigm should recognize that man's evolutionary journey took a detour when so many divine couples chose to consume the fruit of the Tree of Knowledge, the sensual fruit of nature, to satisfy lustful desire. It was a choice to use the knowledge of the energy of the elementals not for good, but for evil. And so, as it is said: we shall know them by their fruits—or by how each divine couple uses the energy of creation.

Only with a new paradigm of thought can it be possible for each of us, as the prodigal sons and daughters of God, to return to the paradise of Eden. It will only be upon our return to Eden that we will once again be clothed in the purity of our immortal physical bodies of light. Make no mistake, the law of balance and harmony that is the hallmark of the consciousness of love ensures that each of us will eventually awaken from our drug-induced sleep. It is simply a matter of waiting out the eons of evolution in front of us or of taking the wheel of evolution and consciously driving, by the shortest route possible, back to Eden. It is really all about the paradigm.

With his life and teachings, Jesus attempted to present man with this new paradigm. However, the sponsors of the paradigm of fear would have nothing of it. When Jesus spoke to the crowds stating: "I and the Father are one" (John 10:30), and "all the things I do you shall also do but even greater" (John 14:12), he was acknowledging that God is not as portrayed by man, a personal and arbitrary ruler over man. He was confirming that God, in his individuated expression as the Christ, as the consciousness of love, resides in each and every one of us. We are, in fact, all children of God, all sons and daughters of God.

The so called second coming does not, as many believe, refer to a second physical appearance of Jesus Christ on Earth, but of the awakening within each of us of the Christ consciousness, of the consciousness of love within our hearts. It is only through a re-awakening to the Christ within his own heart that man can reawaken to his connection to God and be worthy to return to Eden. Until then, Jesus's cry for mercy upon mankind as he hung on the cross will continue to apply: "Father, forgive them for they know not what they do," (Luke 23:34).

We Are All Bound By a Universal Justice

By his actions, man has created a state of disharmony that is incompatible within the perfection of the spirit/matter celestial realm of Eden. By choosing individual self-desire over the unity of love man created a world of imbalance and disharmony. This has led to the appearance of sin and evil in the world. Sin and evil exist not through the acquiescence, and least of all at the direction of God, but solely as a result of the corruption of man's divine consciousness.

Man needs to acknowledge that the infinite conscious love of God is incapable of benign neglect, or of displaying anger, or of inflicting violence upon his children. We need to be honest and to recognize that it is man and not God who allows evil to exist in the world and that man has done so willingly through a corruption of his divine consciousness. Man now has the opportunity to consciously choose love over self-desire and to restore the harmony and balance that he has disturbed within himself and within nature.

In reality, what man fears most is not God but the universal law of justice that inescapably flows out of the exercise of choice. That law requires those who disturb the harmony and balance within creation to restore it. In each and every case justice is meted out by each soul as it stands within the light of its own divine consciousness. There is no third-party intervention—certainly no punishing God.

It is the anticipation of facing the consequences of bad choices, and the requirement of restoring that which has been disturbed that causes mortal man to fear both death and God. The facing of this inescapable justice is what is commonly referred to as karma. Justice or karma is the ultimate and inescapable restorer of balance and harmony. When the scales of justice are upset, creation seeks a restoration of balance from the one who caused the imbalance. Facing justice correlates with man's perception of the wrath of God, of punishment for the sins that we know we have committed, sins that are nothing more than the perpetuation of man's original sin—his deviation from the original plan to further the evolution of the Atom of God Consciousness.

Our freedom of choice has come at a steep price, a price that must be paid. In paying the price we will acquire experience, and with experience we will acquire wisdom, and with wisdom we will move closer to our eventual return to Eden. Man is at that point where collectively he has acquired the necessary wealth of experience and wisdom with which he can consciously choose to restore balance and harmony within himself. In so doing, he will restore the harmonious union, that divine marriage, between the masculine and the feminine consciousness—the marriage that each of us is seeking.

Our temporal reality has become one large classroom. How long we must remain within this classroom is determined by how long it takes each of us to master the curriculum of living a life guided by the consciousness of love. Mastery will not come until we take seriously the purpose of the journey. The temporal world is now the proving ground for souls that would be Gods.

Retracing Our Footsteps

Our decision to consume the forbidden sensual fruit of nature was consciously made; likewise, our decision to return home must also be consciously made. We must once again think as the consciously endowed, immortal expressions of God that we are. We must exercise our latent yet inherent abilities of imaginatively inspired thinking to create a more perfect reality.

Man fell because he chose to experience the sensual within nature. This was a choice of self-desire over love. The result of that choice has been the loss of man's divine consciousness enjoyed within a state of physical immortality. Adam and Eve came to the paradise of Eden as perfect lovers. Their coming together in the experience of love was to be through a union of consciousness. Coming together in this manner is a blissful act, as it is the experience of God within one another. Adam and Eve abandoned their permanent union of conscious love for one another by choosing instead the fleeting sensual experiences within nature.

The road back to the experience of the consciousness of love requires that we first begin by recognizing and embracing our divinity. For too long we have believed that we are our physical bodies. No matter how old, feeble, or infirm we become we often go to extreme lengths to cling to our bodies. Some people have gone so far as to have their bodies frozen in hopes of being revived at a future date when science has discovered ways to prolong life indefinitely.

Religious beliefs have contributed to the assumption that the body is critical by reinforcing the notion that, on judgment day, the righteous shall be raised from the dead and each righteous soul shall be reunited with its own physical body. Many people who oppose cremation believe that if they cremate their body, their soul will not be reunited with their physical body. Explaining that, absent embalming and mummification, a dead physical body turns to dust matters not to those who hold such views.

Clearly, we all want to experience immortality. We all intently want there to be more than one more day or even one hundred years to our existence. But it is not the physical body we should cling to—it is the energy that gives life to the physical body that matters. It is the Atom of God Consciousness clothed with the immortal body of light, and not the physical body of nature that was, is now, and always will be eternal. It is only with the embrace of that reality that we can restore our higher conscious immortality.

The Marriage of Science and Spirituality

Once we have accomplished the first step of recognizing that we are truly more than our physical bodies the next step is to bring about a marriage between science and spirituality. They are, in fact, two halves of the same coin. Science can be seen as the masculine energy and spirituality as the feminine energy of this union. As in any courtship, there must be a foundation of mutual respect and admiration. There must also be a willingness to embrace the principle of surrender. Surrender, in this context, is not submission or a sign of weakness, but rather, a sign of strength. It is simply the ability of each partner to put self-interest aside in order to embrace what the other brings to the union. In the act of surrender, each will find the wholeness of unity.

Science must be willing to put aside its self-interest as reflected in its views on the origin and manifestation of the temporal world and accept the spirit or energy of consciousness as an integral component of the origin of everything. Spirituality, as reflected within religion, must also put aside self-interest in its views on the origin and manifestation of the temporal world and accept evolutionary development as an integral component of the evolution of the spirit of consciousness within matter.

When each partner turns from self-interest and engages one another in a shared consciousness anchored in love, what was once two divided and irreconcilable paths will become one, and a new paradigm will be born.

The Creation of Heaven on Earth

With the marriage of science and spirituality man will have the opportunity to create heaven on earth. Man will eventually pierce the veil between the physical and the non-physical realities. There will be a tangible interaction between the reality of Eden and man, and human society will be profoundly restructured. We will come to realize the greater purpose in this life experience. We will more acutely appreciate the classroom analogy of the temporal worlds and that no soul can possibly complete the necessary lesson plan in a single lifetime. Yes, reincarnation, or re-entering the game of life, is the program we must follow to secure our immortality.

The primary goal to be achieved in the game of life is the right exercise of choice. The right exercise of choice will create no disharmony within the matrix of the temporal world. The wrong exercise of choice, to borrow a phrase from the fictional Star Wars character Obi-Wan Kenobi, will create a disturbance in the force, or within the energetic matrix of the temporal world. There is no element of punishment, certainly not condemnation, in a bad choice. However, as my mother always said, if you are going to sleep in that bed then it is your responsibility to turn it down at night and to turn it up in the morning. If our choices are such as to create a disturbance within the matrix of the world, then it is our responsibility to address head on the disturbances that we have created until we have restored the natural state of harmony. However long it may take to accomplish that goal will determine how many years or lifetime courses we must enroll in before we can graduate. If we remain locked in the cycle of the old paradigm of fear and control, then we can expect to cycle endlessly through lifetime after lifetime. If we can embrace a new paradigm ushered in by the marriage of science and spirituality, then we can expect to more quickly and more successfully complete the lesson plan and return to the paradise of Eden, fully vested with authority to keep and to dress the Garden of Eden.

Conclusion

There Is Joy in the Journey

There are many excellent courses of study available to assist man in the restoration of his higher consciousness. There are many excellent meditation programs designed to help quiet the sense-controlled mind. There are the more advanced step-programs such as found in the Eightfold Path of Buddhism and the Twelve Step Program of Alcoholics Anonymous, each of which provides a concise framework for proper conduct in a world so ripe with temptation and addiction. There are many New Age writings that address in amazing detail the complexities of man as a being of energy resident on multi-dimensional levels of conscious energy.

However, the limitation of all such programs is that they are designed to work within our holographic, and therefore illusionary, reality. Granted, it is essential to have an operational guide for maneuvering within this illusionary reality and to provide a possible exit strategy. These operational guides would be more beneficial if we first had a clear understanding of how we found our way into such a grand virtual reality. In that regard, the current paradigm talks in oversimplified generalities and does not offer the strong underpinnings and foundational support necessary for advancing a successful exit strategy. We cannot find our way out of the illusion and back to our true home without a clear understanding of our real identity and the home we came from.

It is my sincerest hope that this book provides some of that necessary foundational support. However, no matter which program we may adopt, we should do so with the understanding that there is but one road back to Eden and we are all companion travelers on that road. And as companions, we should make this journey with hands reaching out in support of one another. Some will complete the journey in less time than others. Many more will choose to take detours along the way. No matter how long the journey may be for each of us, we should not fail to see the joy along the way.

We should also acknowledge that the disappointments, pain, and suffering that we may suffer along the way are not imposed upon us by either God or our neighbor. Such experiences are simply the consequence of stepping off of the clearly defined path home. Sometimes we stray so far that we become truly lost, and only with great difficulty and the tireless help of others do we find our way back.

Despite the many challenges that we are certain to face in such a long journey, we are still one family united in the love that endlessly flows from the conscious love of God. We should enjoy the successes of one another in the variety of noble and creative endeavors. Such successes are truly a reflection of the God consciousness within each of us. We should most certainly enjoy our connections with family and friends; the milestone celebrations of birthdays, graduations, marriages, and even the pull of love as loved ones set out on their own life journeys. By so enjoying life, by collectively holding hands in a shared love for one another, we may be surprised at how short we can make the journey back to Eden.

There Will Be More on This Conversation to Follow

I wrote *Dying to Be Immortal* in an effort to bring about a change in the conversation of our understanding of man's origin—his relationship to God and his experience within this temporal world reality. Given the expansion of man's conscious awareness and psychic development within just the past several decades, current assumptions as to man's origin and his placement within this reality seem parochial at best.

It is my sincerest wish to continue this conversation and to that end I am writing two additional books. These written conversations are intended to provide a broad alternative view to the questions pertaining to man's origin, his fall from grace, his ultimate redemption and victorious return to Eden. I believe that without consideration of an alternative to the current paradigm we will continue to live our lives not only in ignorance of the greater reality of our conscious immortality, but also of our true relationship to God.

For far too long man has been blinded to his true reality, by his addiction to the sensual experience of living within nature. As a result, any genuine search for answers to experiences transcending normal or physical human experience has been severely handicapped. Failing to understand that we are much more than the collective of sensations generated within our physical bodies is like trying to solve a puzzle with only half of the necessary pieces. I hope that my small contribution helps in locating some of the missing pieces of the puzzle.

The working title of my second book is *On the Road to Eden: Conversations with My Children*. One cannot witness the innocence and joy expressed in the smile of a child and not be profoundly affected. Our children give us a window into the soul that we most often fail to look into. If we but looked with sincerity and a little inspired imagination, we would see the reflections of Eden within their bright little faces. If we did so, we would be more attentive to our role as parents and teachers in fostering within each child the ability to access his/her maximum potential for living life as an expression of the divine consciousness that they are. In becoming parents we agreed to provide a doorway to a soul transiting from Eden to Earth to complete their evolutionary journey. And to those children born to us we agreed to sponsor their physical and spiritual development as nurturers and teachers. It is an appreciation of those commitments that has formed the catalyst for this book. It is my sincere hope that the continuing conversations within this book will speak to what all parents wish to convey to their children about the experience of life as a divine and immortal soul.

Where my first book deals with our origin as immortal souls, and my second book with guidance for the soul's journey while on Earth, my third book, *At the Gates of Eden: Journey's End*, will discuss death and our return home to Eden.

If nothing else, it is my hope that this book will allow us to face our inevitable deaths with as much anticipation as that with which we welcomed all of the other positive experiences within our lives. Fear need not be our companion as we prepare to return home to Eden. Death is nothing more than the cessation of sensations within the physical body. It is simply nature's way of cycling life within its realm. Having fallen into nature, we are bound by its laws. In death, we all receive a much-deserved period of rest and the joyful embrace of the family and friends who have gone before us.

More importantly, as each Adam and Eve we will have the opportunity to once again come together in that blissful union of love. It is the joy and bliss of that reunion that continues to propel us back to Earth, lifetime after lifetime, in the effort to achieve that final redemption and the passage through death for the very last time.

Acknowledgments

I wish to give a special acknowledgment to Jeannette Waugh, Bonnie Bowen, Tom and Jenn Bete-Brown, Gail Ingalls, Rod Kurtz, Kara and Kristie Langone, Mickey Russo, Jim and Kathy Parker, and Lynn Rockwell for their creative support and critical commentary in what was for me a most personal journey.

A special thank you goes to my wife, Maureen. It is only from a spouse that you can receive a loving yet unvarnished assessment of your work. She was invaluable in redirecting me when necessary with recommendations to change a word here or a sentence there or with a simple, "Honey, just delete this whole section."

I am most thankful to my children, Ethan and Shannon. The reality of the divine within each of us is most easily seen through the eyes of a child. The reason children are so embraceable is because they have not yet learned how to be human. For a period of time they remain clothed in a garment of angelic light. If we look close enough, and embrace our children with open hearts, we can see and touch the face of God.

Finally, I owe a special acknowledgment to Julie Andrés (Jools) of Blue Moon Publishing for taking the fabric of my raw manuscript and, with skillful application, turning it into a book.

Resources

The Science of Metaphysics

Adyashanti (1962 –), *The Collected Works of Adyashanti: Emptiness Dancing* (Adyashanti, 2006), *Spontaneous Awakening* (Adyashanti, 2005), *My Secret is Silence* (Adyashanti, 2003), and *The Impact of Awakening* ((Adyashanti, 2002). Adyashanti offers spontaneous and direct nondual teachings that have been compared to those of the early Zen masters and Advaita Vedanta sages. "The liberating truth is not static; it is alive. It cannot be put into concepts and be understood by the mind. The truth lies beyond all forms of conceptual fundamentalism." www.adyashanti.org

William Boulting (1897 – 1975), *Giordano Bruno, His Life, Thought, and Martyrdom*, (Kegan Paul, Trench, Trubner & Co., 1914).

Richard Maurice Bucke (1837 – 1902), MD, *Cosmic Consciousness: A Study in the Evolution of the Human Mind* (E.P. Dutton & Co., Inc., 1969). A classic investigation of the development of man's mystic relation to the infinite.

Carlos Castaneda (1925 – 1998). Castaneda often referred to what he called nonordinary reality, a realm that was radically different from the reality experienced by most human beings who, as part of their social conditioning, are preoccupied with their everyday activities. www.castaneda.com

Ernest Holmes (1887 – 1960), et al, *The Collected Works of Ernest Holmes, Charles Fillmore* (1854 – 1948), *William Walker Atkinson* (1862 – 1932), *James Allen* (1864 – 1912), *and Henry Drummond* (1851 – 1897). Pioneers in The New Thought Movement, a spiritual movement that developed in the United States during the late 19th century and emphasizes metaphysical beliefs that promote the idea that God is ubiquitous, that divinity dwells within each person, that we are all spiritual beings, and that the highest spiritual principle [is] loving one another unconditionally. www.newthoughtlibrary.com

Boris Mouravieff (1890 – 1966), *Gnosis: Study and Commentaries on The Esoteric Tradition of Eastern Orthodoxy; The Exoteric Cycle Cycle(Vol. I), The Mesoteric Cycle (Vol II); and The Esoteric Cycle (Vol. III)*. (Praxis Institute Press, Chicago, IL, 1992, 1989, 1993, respectively).

Harold W. Percival (1868 – 1963). In 1893 Percival had the unique experience of being "conscious of consciousness," a potent spiritual and noetic enlightenment. He stated: "Being conscious of consciousness reveals the 'unknown' to the one who has been so conscious. Then it will be the duty of that one to make known what he can of being conscious of consciousness." His works represent a towering accomplishment in addressing the true state, and potential, of the human. His complete system of thinking is contained in a one-thousand-page masterpiece, produced over a period of thirty-four years and entitled *Thinking and Destiny*, first published in 1946, © The Word Foundation. www.thewordfoundation.org

Dr. Helen Schucman (1909 – 1981) and Dr. William Thetford (1923 – 1988), *A Course in Miracles* (Foundation for Inner Peace, 1975). Describing a purely non-dualistic approach to spirituality, ACIM integrates ideas from Christianity, Eastern religions, mysticism, psychology, and Platonism, viewing reality as monistically consisting of a single thing, the love of God, and the physical world as a projection in the mind. ACIM focuses on cultivating awareness of love in the self and in others. www.acim.org

Rudolph Steiner (1861 – 1925). An Austrian philosopher, literary scholar, educator, artist, playwright, social thinker, and mystic, Steiner offers a spiritual philosophy he called anthroposophy. HE postulates the existence of an objective, intellectually comprehensible, spiritual world accessible to direct experience through inner development, more specifically through conscientiously cultivating a form of thinking independent of sensory experience. In its investigations of the spiritual world, anthroposophy aims to attain the precision and clarity of natural science's investigations of the physical world. Steiner's books are available at www.rsarchive.org

Emanuel Swedenborg (1688 – 1772). a Swedish scientist, philosopher, theologian and Christian mystic best known for his book Heaven and Hell, first published in Latin in 1758, in which he offers a detailed description of the afterlife. www.swedenborg.org

Pierre Teilhard de Chardin (1881 – 1955),A French philosopher and Jesuit priest, Teilhard sets forth a sweeping account of the unfolding of the cosmos in his primary book *The Phenomenon of Man* (Editions de Seuil, Paris, 1955). He abandoned traditional interpretations of creation in the Book of Genesis in favor of a less strict interpretation. In *The Future of Man* ((Editions de Seuil, Paris, 1959), Teilhard presents his philosophy and belief that man is evolving spiritually from a simple faith to a higher form of consciousness, including a Consciousness of God. In 1925, Teilhard was ordered by the Jesuit Superior General to leave his teaching position in France and to sign a statement withdrawing his controversial statements regarding the doctrine of original sin. This was the first in a series of condemnations by certain church officials, with the climax of these condemnations with a 1962 monitum (reprimand) of the Holy Office denouncing his works. See information regarding his collected works at www.teilharddechardin.org

Eckhart Tolle (1948 –) presents an honest look at the current state of humanity and argues that this state, which is based on an erroneous identification with the egocentric mind, is one of dangerous insanity. He believes that the feeding of the human ego is the source of inner and outer conflict and that only in examining one's ego may people begin to see beyond it and obtain a sense of spiritual enlightening or a new outlook on reality. Books include *A New Earth* (Penguin, 2006), *The Power of Now* (New World Library, 2004), and

Stillness Speaks (New World Library, 2003). www.eckharttolle.com

Alan Wilson Watts (1915 – 1973). A British philosopher, writer, speaker, and student of comparative religion, Watts was best known as an interpreter and popularizer of Asian philosophies for a Western audience. He wrote more than 25 books and numerous articles on subjects such as personal identity, the true nature of reality, higher consciousness, the meaning of life, concepts and images of God, and the nonmaterial pursuit of happiness. In his books he relates his experience to scientific knowledge and to the teachings of Eastern and Western religion and philosophy. www.alanwatts.com

Gary Zukav (1942 –), *The Mind of the Soul: Responsible Choice* (Free Press, 2003) with co-author Linda Francis; *The Heart of the soul: Emotional Awareness* (Simon and Schuster, 2002), co-author Linda Francis; *Soul Stories* (Free Press, 2000); *The Seat of the Soul* (Free Press, 1989); and *The Dancing Wu Li Masters: An Overview of the New Physics* (Bantam, 1979). www.zukav.com

The Science of Consciousness

Itzhak Bentov (1923 – 1979), *A Brief Tour of Higher Consciousness* (Destiny Books, 2000), and *Stalking the Wild Pendulum* (Destiny Books, 1977). Bentov was a Czech-born scientist, inventor, mystic, author, and an early exponent of what has come to be referred to as consciousness studies.

Robert Allan Monroe (1915 – 1995). In 1975 Monroe registered a patent for an audio-visual device designed to stimulate brain functions until the left and right hemispheres became synchronized. Monroe held that this state, dubbed Hemi-Sync (hemispherical synchronization), could be used to promote mental well-being or to trigger an altered state of consciousness. He is credited with popularizing the term "out-of-body experience". His books include *Journeys Out of the Body* (Broadway Books, 1971), *Far Journeys* (Broadway Books, 1992), and *Ultimate Journey* (Three Rivers Press, 1996). www.monroeinstitute.com

Russell Targ (1934 –). An American physicist and author and an ESP researcher, Targ conducted research into psychic abilities and operational use of these abilities that he and his colleague collectively referred to as "remote viewing." www.espresearch.com

Charles T. Tart, PhD. (1937 –). Dr. Tart is an American psychologist and parapsychologist known for his work on the nature of consciousness (particularly altered states of consciousness), as one of the founders of the field of transpersonal psychology, and for his research in scientific parapsychology. www.paradigm-sys.com/cttart/

Ken Wilber (1949 –) is founder of the Integral Institute, and formulator of the "integral theory of consciousness." He is a leading proponent of the integral movement (also called the integral paradigm, integral philosophy, the integral worldview, or the integral approach), a movement that seeks a comprehensive understanding of humans and the universe by combining, among other things, scientific and spiritual insights. www.kenwilber.com

Institute of Noetic Science – a nonprofit organization that conducts and sponsors leading-edge research into the potentials and powers of consciousness—including perceptions, beliefs, attention, intention, and intuition. The Institute explores phenomena that do not necessarily fit conventional scientific models, while maintaining a commitment to scientific rigor. www.noetic.org

What the BLEEP Do We Know? (2004). A documentary blending quantum physics, spirituality, mysticism, science, neurology, and evolutionary thought in a new type of film; part documentary, part story, with elaborate and inspiring visual effects and animations. www.whatthebleep.com

The Science of Reincarnation

Deepak Chopra, MD (1946 –). Chopra tells us that there is abundant evidence that "the world beyond" is not separated from this world by an impassable wall; in fact, a single reality embraces all worlds, all times and places. Ultimately, there is no division between life and death. At the end of our lives, we "cross over" into a new phase of the same soul journey we are on right this minute. In his book, *Life After Death* (Random House, 2006) Chopra draws on cutting-edge scientific discoveries and the great wisdom traditions to provide a map of the afterlife. It's a fascinating journey into many levels of consciousness. But far more important is his urgent message: "Who you meet in the afterlife and what you experience there reflect your present beliefs, expectations, and level of awareness. In the here and now you can shape what happens after you die." www.chopra.com

Raymond Moody, MD. (1944 –), *Life After Life* (Harper, San Francisco, 2002). Author of books about life after death and near-death experiences (NDE), a term that he coined in 1975, Moody's bestselling book investigates the phenomenon of survival of bodily death. www.lifeafterlife.com

Michael Newton, PhD (1951 –). Founder of the Dr. Michael Newton Institute for Life Between Lives, and author of the best-selling books *Journey of Souls* (Llewellyn, St. Paul, MN, 1994), *Destiny of Souls* (Llewellyn, 2000), and *Life Between Lives* (Llewellyn, 2004). www.michaelnewtonphd.com

Sogyal Rinpoche (1947 –), *Tibetan Book of Living and Dying* (HarperCollins, 1992). Gives a comprehensive presentation of the teachings of Tibetan Buddhism and explores the message of impermanence, evolution, karma, rebirth, the practice of compassion, how to care for and show love to the dying, and spiritual practices for the moment of death. Rinpoche says: "What is it I hope for from this book? To inspire a quiet revolution in the whole way we look at death and care for the dying and the whole way we look at life, and care for the living." usa.rigpa.org

Brian Weiss, MD (1944 –), *Same Soul, Many Bodies* (Free Press, a division of Simon and S, 2004). In this astounding book, Weiss, one of the first doctors to explore the past lives of his patients as a means of therapy, reveals how past and present lives can affect our future lives, and how our future lives can transform us in the here and now. "We have all lived past lives. All of us will live future ones. What we do in this life will influence our lives to come as we evolve toward immortality." www.brianweiss.com

The Science of the Universe

Herbert Friedman (1916 – 2009), *The Astronomer's Universe: Stars, Galaxies, and Cosmos* (W W Norton & Co Inc., 1998).

Brian Greene (19 –), *The Elegant Universe: Superstrings, Hidden Dimensions, and the Quest for the Ultimate Theory* (W W Norton & Co Inc., 2003). Greene is known as a theoretical physicist and author.

John Gribbin (1946 –), *The Birth of Time: How We Measured the Age of the Universe* (Weidenfeld & Nicolson, 1998).

Stephen Hawking (1942 –), *A Brief History of Time* (Bantam Dell, 1998).

Religion

Willis Barnstone (1927 –) and Marvin Meyer (1948 –), ed. *The Gnostic Bible* (New Seed, an imprint of Shambhala Publications, Inc., Boston, MA.) www.shambhala.com

The Holy Bible: Douay-Rheims Version, World eBook Library PGCC Collection; *The Old Testament*, first Published by the English College at Douay, 1609 and 1610; *The New Testament*, First Published by the English College at Rheims, 1582. www.WorldLibrary.net

Archbishop Wake (1657 – 1737), *Forbidden Books of the Original New Testament* (http://www.gutenberg.org Ebook #6516). The suppressed gospels and epistles of the original New Testament of Jesus the Christ and other portions of the ancient holy scriptures. Now extant, attributed to his apostles and their disciples, and venerated by the primitive Christian churches during the first four centuries, but, after violent disputations, forbidden by the bishops of the Nicene Council in the reign of the Emperor Constantine and omitted from the Catholic and Protestant editions of the New Testament.

Other Resources

Inspired Imagination

Randy Pausch (1960 – 2008). *The Last Lecture: Really Achieving Your Childhood Dreams,* delivered at Carnegie Mellon University, September 18, 2007; available at www.cmu.edu/randyslecture/

Randy Pausch and Jeffrey Zaslow (1958 –) *The Last Lecture*, (Hyperion Books, 2009).

The Consciousness of Love

W. L. Garver (dates of birth and death unknown). *Brother of the Third Degree* (Borden Publishing Company, 1964; first copyrighted in 1894 by W. L. Garver). www.sacred-texts.com

Frederick S. Oliver (1866 – 1899), *A Dweller on Two Planets,* by Phylos the Thibetan. www.sacred-texts.com

We Are Not Alone

Zecharia Sitchin (1920 – 2010) *The Collected Works of Zecharia Sitchin.* www.sitchin.com

Author's Note

Throughout this book I often referred to God in the masculine. I could have just as easily referred to God in the feminine. However, there is no pronoun in the human language that is a suitable substitute when referring to the all-encompassing power and presence we call God. The reality is God is both masculine and feminine at the same time.

About the Author

Dan Brown's interest in metaphysics was sparked when as a teenager he read *The Sleeping Prophet*, the life story of Edgar Cayce. In it he found a fascinating presentation of a reality existing outside of the world most of us know and experience. The exciting concepts of *The Sleeping Prophet*, particularly that of the existence of a higher conscious reality, led him in the 1970s to pursue the study of philosophy and metaphysics at Boston College.

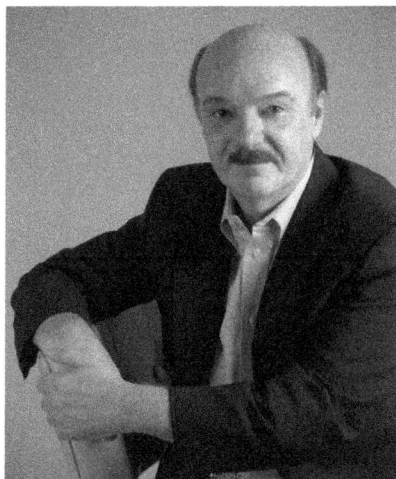

A lifetime of study of the writings of ancient and modern-day philosophers such as Plato, Nietzsche, and Steiner, and of scientific writers such as Einstein and Hawking has guided him on his journey in search for the essential reality behind the world of visible form.

Dan is a lawyer and lives with his wife and two children in Concord, NH. He welcomes your comments and can be contacted by email at:

eden.chronicles@gmail.com

Or by writing to:

The Eden Chronicles
P.O. Box 697
Concord, NH 03302

www.ingramcontent.com/pod-product-compliance
Lightning Source LLC
Chambersburg PA
CBHW031955040426
42448CB00006B/370